A Year with Yours

Name	
Address	
Postcode	
Home phone	
Mobile phone	
Email	

In case of emergency, contact:

Name	
Telephone	

USEFUL CONTACTS

BANK	
BUILDING SOCIETY	
CHEMIST/PHARMACY	
CHIROPODIST	
COUNCIL	
CREDIT CARD EMERGENCY	
DENTIST	
DOCTOR	
ELECTRICIAN	
GARAGE	
HAIRDRESSER	
HOSPITAL	
LOCAL POLICE	
MILKMAN	
OPTICIAN	
PLUMBER	
SOLICITOR	
TAXI	
VET	

RENEWAL REMINDERS

	RENEWAL DATE	POLICY NUMBER	TELEPHONE
CAR INSURANCE			
CAR TAX			
MOT			
HOME INSURANCE			
TV LICENCE			
PET INSURANCE			
Yours SUBSCRIPTION			

The year ahead

In their mother's wake

Spring signals new life in the countryside, as fresh shoots burst from the ground and tiny eggs, that have been huddled in the warmth of nests, begin to hatch. For a mallard, this happens approximately 28 days after the beginning of incubation. The ducklings will stay in the nest for at least 10 hours, while they become accustomed to their legs. Then they will begin their journey into the water. Their first voyage usually occurs early in the morning. Once on the water, you'll see the ducklings gliding in a long line behind their mother, and they will remain here by her side for 50-60 days before they fledge and become independent.

Garden jobs

Simple steps to keep your plot looking good this season

BOOST NEXT YEAR'S DAFFS

After your daffodils have finished flowering, pick off the developing seedheads – they snap off between finger and thumb in a very satisfying way! Leave the foliage to die back naturally then lightly rake some rose fertiliser (try Toprose, £3.95/1kg, wilko.com) into the soil to give them a boost for the best blooms next year.

Jump-start dahlias

Plant tubers indoors now for longer-blooming, healthier plants. Place in pots of multipurpose compost with the crowns just below the compost. Water well and keep the compost moist. Place on a windowsill then plant out in a sunny spot in May.

OUTWIT SLUGS

As temperatures rise and your plants start growing again, slugs and snails wake up too. They aren't fussy about what they eat and most plants will be on the menu! Slugs love citrus, so leave fresh orange and lemon peel around your garden to tempt them away.

In the morning, collect up the pests and rehome them on a patch of waste ground, or drop them into a bucket of hot, salty water.

PERFECT YOUR SWEET PEAS

There are two secrets to beautiful sweet peas. First, water whenever the compost starts to feel dry to the touch. And, for lots more blooms, pinch off the tip of the growing stem when the plants are at least 10cm tall. This will encourage them to grow lots more flower-laden stems.

BAG A BARGAIN

Look out for snowdrop bulbs 'in the green' in nurseries or online. These are bulbs that have bloomed and are dug up just after they've finished flowering.

They're cheap as chips and will flower better next spring than bulbs planted in autumn. Plant 10cm deep in a shady spot and water thoroughly to ensure they settle in well.

REVIVE YOUR LAWN

Mow when it's dry with blades on the highest setting then gradually lower them as spring gets fully underway. To repair any bald patches, scatter over a seed-and-feed, such as Patch Magic (£10/1kg, wilko.com).

LET YOUR DANDELIONS BEE

It may be tempting to dig the dandelions out of your lawn but try to leave a few to flower because they're full of pollen and nectar, and bees and butterflies love 'em!

Get more blooms from patio roses

Snip off twiggy branches then cut main stems back by one-third to a healthy bud. Feed with a rose fertiliser (try Toprose, £3.95/1kg, wilko.com), which contains high levels of potash to give blooms a boost, as well as trace elements to keep leaves healthy and help prevent diseases.

Spring into action!

Emerge from your winter hibernation and make the most of the new season by getting active outdoors

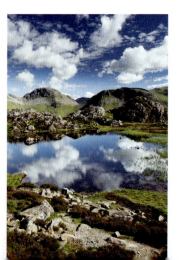

WALK WITH WONDER

There's nothing like a good walk to put a spring in your step. It won't just make you feel physically fitter but has been proven to give a mental boost. The Lake District is synonymous with walking, but you don't have to conquer any peaks to experience all its beauty. Lake Buttermere (meaning 'lake by the dairy pasture') has an easy and level path which winds its way around for a full four-and-a-half mile lap of the lake, taking in waterfalls, meadows and woodlands and even going through rocky tunnels. The best bits, though, are the views of the crystal-clear lake and the impressive peaks of Fleetwith Pike and Haystacks, which was Alfred Wainright's favourite. For more details see lakedistrict.gov.uk

Go wild and swim

As soon as the first spring bulbs appear, there's a little warmth in the sun and the days are that bit longer, it's time to brave the water. Whether you're after an exhilarating quick plunge, a sedate swim or something more energetic, the Brecon Beacons has plenty of options (an area now officially known of course as 'Bannau Brycheiniog').

Lady Falls, also known as Sgwd Gwladys, is set in a natural amphitheatre and is surrounded by woodland. To get there, from the village of Pontneddfechan, take a 30-minute walk along the riverside Elidir trail. You'll be rewarded with a spectacular seven-metre waterfall as well as a beautiful pool to swim in.

GET GOLFING

More than a third of golfers in the UK are women and more and more of us are discovering it later in life, and loving the health benefits it brings (strengthening muscles and improving balance). Of course, there's a lot to be said for spending hours outside in the fresh air too, soaking up your surroundings. Taking part in a women's golfing break is a great way to enjoy a game or two, meet other women and explore a new area. For instance, The Ladies Collection has a one-night half-board stay at Formby Hall Golf Resort and Spa, including two rounds of golf from £110, see theladiescollection.co.uk

CYCLE THE CITIES

Cycling is fantastic for improving your strength and balance. It's a low impact activity but it's also great at allowing you to explore more of an area than you would on foot. The Bristol and Bath Railway Path is a smooth, wide, tree-lined path that stretches 16 miles along the former track, allowing you to take in former stations, disused mills and a selection of sculptures. If you work up an appetite, stop at Warmley and Bitton stations, which both have cafes, and of course there's plenty to do in the cities at either end. If it's been a while since you cycled, hire an e-bike and catch the train for the return leg! For more see sustrans.org.uk

Mess about on the river

In all its shapes and forms, boating provides a fun way to explore an area. The Victorians introduced boating to the Norfolk Broads and, since then, generations have been taking in the breathtaking landscape, plentiful wildlife and enjoying a relaxed pace of life. If you like to keep active, try canoeing, kayaking or paddleboarding – this allows you to explore some of the quieter waterways and you can choose anything from a half-day tour to a three-day camp. Sailing is an exhilarating way to take in your surroundings or, for something more sedate, hire a cruiser. See visitthebroads.co.uk

Fragile flowers

Decorate your home
with these pretty floral
painted eggs

*Gather your materials – if
you want to mix your own
colours grab an old plate to
use as a mixing palette*

All materials available
from Hobbycraft.co.uk

You will need...
Various paintbrushes
A paint palette or old plate
Gouache poster paint in
various colours
Ceramic eggs

1 For the first design you will need to paint three large teardrops that all join at the same point. You can see this will make up your first floral motif. Colour in with your paints.

2 Repeat this shape opposite in a smaller size then, taking another colour, paint two lines that curve from the bottom of the flower. Add leaf shapes along the lines.

3 Repeat this to create a bunch of foliage that gathers between the floral motifs. Once your layers are dry you can add detail, such as lighter highlight on the floral petals.

4 Paint small lines that make up bud branches, working outwards from your florals. These can be painted with singular brush stroke lines and dabs of colour for the buds.

1 This second design uses the same teardrop-style florals (group three together that join at the bottom). You'll need to paint smaller to create a ditsy style. Repeat across your egg.

2 Using single line strokes add the stems with another colour of the gouache paint. Remember to point your stems in different directions to create movement in the design.

1 This next design creates textured petals. Don't use too much water, and have a thicker consistency of gouache so you can press down and use the bristles to make petal shapes. Repeat over the egg.

2 Using another colour pop a dot into the centre of your floral shapes to create a ditsy style of pattern.

1 For this motif design paint a five-petal floral. Simply paint ovals that all join together around an imaginary circle in the middle.

2 Add delicate leaf shapes in another colour. These should work outwards from your floral shapes.

3 Using another colour add a circle shape to the centre of your petals to create your pretty floral motifs.

Your beautifully painted eggs are now ready to display!

Summer's soft light

The lingering warmth of late summer makes a countryside walk all the more pleasurable, especially when the sun is low in the sky. At this quieter time of day, the beauty of the season can still be enjoyed without the busyness of crowds, and favoured routes take on new perspective as the countryside is transformed by the changing light of the sun's descent. Wildlife that may be hiding during the day, such as the elusive nightjar or the nightingale, may be glimpsed in the stillness of the evening, emerging from their hideaways at dusk. The glorious pinks and yellows of the sunset can be admired as they tint the landscape in a golden glow before it is succeeded by the silver light of the moon.

Garden jobs

Simple steps to keep your plot looking good this season

HYDRATE PLANTS TO HAPPINESS

In summer, water thirsty plants early morning or late evening when it's cooler so they have time to drink before it evaporates. Soaking the soil 1-2 times a week, and adding Flower Power Plant Food (£14.99/475g, dobies.co.uk), rather than watering every day, will make them more drought resistant. Finish with a layer of grass clippings around shrubs to help seal in moisture.

Keep pots perky

Water daily to keep the compost moist using a watering can or hosepipe on a gentle flow. If you're going away, set up a self-watering kit that connects to a tap with a timer. Try Hozelock 15 Pot Watering Kit, £36.99, hayesgardenworld.co.uk.

Make baby pelargoniums

They're easy to grow from cuttings. Snip off a shoot just above a leaf joint, trim the bottom just below a leaf joint and remove leaves from the lower two thirds. Add to a 7.5cm pot of Sowing & Cutting Compost (£2.50, wilko.com), water and stand on a shady cool windowsill. When roots are growing out the drainage holes, move it into a bigger pot.

Summer gardening

Make cut blooms last for longer

To get the best out of them in a vase, cut flowers early in the morning as this is when they are most hydrated. Cut the stems with sharp secateurs just as the buds begin to open and put them straight into a vase of clean water.

Help hedgehogs

Our prickly garden friends can get dehydrated in dry warm spells so leave out a shallow dish of water for them to drink.

SOAK IN A DELICIOUS SUMMER SCENT

Add a pot of lavender to your patio and let its aromatic cloud carry your worries away every time you settle down outside. Plant in peat-free compost with added John Innes and this sun lover won't care a jot if you forget to water it sometimes. Try lavender 'Pink Summer Improved' (£12.99/5 plants, thompson-morgan.com) for gorgeous rose pink blooms well into September.

RESTORE YOUR ROPEY RATTAN

If you have an old piece of rattan furniture that is looking worse for wear, rub some olive oil over it using a soft cloth. This will reduce cracking and add shine, making it look as good as new.

PAD OUT YOUR GARDEN POND

Now's a great time to get pond plants going so they settle in and grow over summer. Waterlilies look good and add shelter and shade for fish and wildlife. Try the Waterlily Planting Kit, £21.99, yougarden.com.

Seaside eats

From licking an ice cream while dipping your toes in the surf to delighting in fresh cockles as the evening sun warms your face, the UK seaside offers some classic British foodie experiences

THE MAGPIE CAFE, WHITBY

More than just a fish 'n' chippie, the Magpie is a Yorkshire landmark that's been a cafe since 1939 and won award after award. The distinctive black and white former merchant's house overlooks the harbour, offering fabulous views of Whitby.

As well as top-notch fish and chips, you can order the likes of seafood chowder, Whitby crab bisque, fish pie, calamari or create your own fish platter. You can book a table in the famous café or join the queue and get a takeaway to eat in the sea air before visiting the ruins of Whitby Abbey and seeing if you can conquer the 199 steps – like Dracula – for great views over the harbour and town. For more see magpiecafe.co.uk.

Wiveton Hall Cafe, Norfolk

On the north Norfolk coast near Blakeney, Wiveton Hall is a 17th century, Dutch gabled house with a cafe, shop and holiday cottages. The colourful café serves breakfast (including full English, eggs Benedict and homemade granola), the likes of salads and Cromer crab sandwiches for lunch and, at the weekends, has Italian themed evenings. There are views out across the salt marshes and of Cley Windmill, and there's plenty to do in this Area of Outstanding Beauty, from watching grey seals at Blakeney Point in the nature reserve to walking the Norfolk Coast Path. See wivetonhall.co.uk for more information.

MOOMAID OF ZENNOR, CORNWALL

When you're in Cornwall, a Mr Whippy doesn't quite cut it. Moodmaid's makes luxury Cornish ice cream on its family-run dairy farm and sells it in delis, shops, hotels and restaurants, plus in its two ice cream parlours – in St Ives and the small village of Porthtowan. The latter is on Beach Road, making it the perfect incentive once you've finished building your sandcastle.

Ice creams are made using clotted cream or cream and flavours can be as simple and satisfying as vanilla bean or Cornish clotted cream and honeycomb, or more exciting combinations such as salted almond and hazelnut praline and prosecco sorbet. See moomaidofzennor.com for more.

The Ship Inn, Elie, Fife

In the heart of the seaside resort of Elie, on the east-central coast of Scotland, the Ship Inn overlooks flat, golden sands. It's attained the delightfully niche claim to fame that it's the only pub in Britain to have a cricket team with a pitch on the beach (make a beeline to watch a match on Saturdays during the summer). Food-wise, fill up on pub classics such as Fife beef burgers or fish and chips, followed by Arran ice cream before walking the Fife coastal path or exploring the harbours of Crail, Anstruther or Pittenweem. There are also six bedrooms in the pub, should you fancy extending your stay. For more see shipinn.scot.

THE LOBSTER SHACK, WHITSTABLE

The three-mile Whitstable Coastal Trail passes Whitstable Castle & Gardens and a historic 43-foot wooden Oyster Yawl. But head for the end of the East Quay in the harbour for The Lobster Shack, a beach bar that serves delicious seafood and local wines, as well as its own beer, plus offers stunning sea views over the Thames Estuary.

Whitstable oysters are a must, especially as The Lobster Shack farms their own, but there are also tempting mixed platters and a lobster menu available. There's plenty of outdoor seating, plus live music at the weekends. To find out more see thelobstershack.co.uk.

Iced delights!

*These colourful ice cream cake pops
are delicious and so easy to make*

All materials available from Hobbycraft.co.uk

You will need..
400g tub readymade butter cream icing
12 readymade sponge cupcakes
8 food safe lollipop sticks
Deco melts in the following colours:
Purple, blue, white and pink
Edible sprinkles

1 Crumble the sponge cupcakes into fine crumbs in a bowl. Stir in the buttercream icing a teaspoon at a time until the mixture is thick and holds together when squeezed in your hand.

2 Line a baking tray with greaseproof paper. Divide the mixture into eight and use your hands to squeeze and mould the mixture into ice lolly shapes. Lay them down on the lined tray and insert a lolly stick into each one. Put the tray of cake pops into the freezer until they are solid – this should take approximately an hour.

3 Melt the coloured Deco Melts in a bowl over a pan of hot water. Remove the cake pops from the freezer and submerge each one into the melted Deco Melts to cover. Lay them back down on the tray to set.

4 Melt the white Deco Melts and have some sprinkles to hand. Use a teaspoon to drizzle a small amount at the top of each cake pop and encourage it to drip down. Add sprinkles to the white Deco Melts before it sets. Continue working in this way until each of the cake pops has been decorated.

Ridges on the shore

Beautiful Britain

The mellow light of autumn bathes the cliffs of Bantham Beach
in a golden radiance. Nestled on the Devonshire coast, the
beach is situated at the mouth of the meandering River Avon
and is part of the designated South Devon Area of Outstanding
Natural Beauty. From the shore, Bigbury Bay and the iconic
landmark Burgh Island can be seen on the horizon. Sheltered
by sandy dunes, the beach features a spectacular mass of rock
fragments, ledges and ridges that appear as the tide recedes and
are illuminated in ribbons of light by the evening sun.

Garden jobs

Simple steps to keep your plot looking good this season

Clear away nuisance leaves

Remove fallen leaves from your lawn straight away or they'll make the grass underneath go brown. They can also make paving slippery, so sweep them off your patio. Rake them into piles, then two pieces of cardboard can be used as grabbers to scoop them up and put them in your green garden waste bin.

Autumn gardening

Protect delicate plants with a fleecy coat

Keep an eye on the weather forecast and, at the first mention of frosts, wrap not-so-tough plants, such as cordylines and pittosporums, in horticultural fleece (£14.99/20m, waitrosegarden.com) to keep them insulated. Remove if mild weather returns but replace again in cold spells.

SAVOUR SEEDHEADS

Your allium seedheads will be looking fab right about now. While you'll no doubt want to leave a few of them in place for insects to hunker down in over winter, and also because they look stunning, particularly covered in a frosty glaze in winter, why not snip a few of the rest and arrange them in a vase indoors where they'll last for months, if not years?

ADD SPRING ZING

Brighten up a dreary autumn day by heading to a garden centre for some wallflowers. They're often sold in bunches or planted in small pots. Pop them in a sunny spot now where they'll grow slowly then burst into life in spring with zingy flowers and sweet scent.

SPRUCE UP FLOWERBEDS

Use sharp secateurs to trim drooping straggly stems of any remaining summer plants down to the ground. Remove plant supports, wipe over and store them away for next summer.

BUFF YOUR BUTT

Give your water butt a yearly clean ready for the autumn rains to fill it up, and to stop its contents stagnating. Empty it, scrub inside using a mix of half a cup each of white vinegar and water and 1tsp lemon juice, rinsing it afterwards. Cover with a meshed lid to stop leaves getting in, if needs be.

PUT OUT PEANUTS

They're loved by tits, finches, starlings and more and they're extra high energy – needed for the colder months.

Squeeze in a shrub or two

If that flowerbed bare spot has been niggling at you, now's the time to fill it, while the soil is still warm and moist, and before any winter weather wobbles. We love evergreen Mexican orange blossom (£22.99/2L pot, crocus.co.uk) for its starry white blooms in May and late summer.

Make for the city

Autumn is the perfect time for a city break – the days are still light and warm enough to spend wandering around, but when it's cold outside, our cities offer world-class attractions

BELFAST

This small city has a thriving arts scene, cosy pubs and a fascinating history to explore. The Titanic Belfast Museum is filled with interactive exhibitions – afterwards be sure to walk along the harbour or, for something a little further, head up Cave Hill (also known as Napoleon's nose) and take in Belfast Castle.

A Belfast Black Taxi tour will take you through divided neighbourhoods, where you'll learn about The Troubles and see the political murals. More street art is at CS Lewis Square, a homage to the Narnia creator.

In the evening, the Cathedral Quarter is the place for live music and a Guinness. The Grand Opera House showcases West End and Broadway shows, while the Modern Arts Centre is great for independent productions.
■ Rooms at the Bullitt Hotel start at £89, bullitthotel.com

VIBRANT LIVERPOOL

Steeped in maritime history, no trip to Liverpool is complete without a wander around the Royal Albert Dock. Once one of the world's most important ports, it's now home to top class museums and galleries, including the Maritime Museum, the International Slavery Museum, Tate Liverpool, and The Beatles Story, which includes a full-size replica of The Cavern Club plus George Harrison's first guitar. Take a ferry across the Mersey to the Wirral (you'll not be able to resist singing the tune!) for a tour, and return to visit the Neo-Gothic Liverpool Cathedral, Britain's largest church (on a clear day you can see Blackpool Tower from its tower). Then try to catch a performance at the art deco Philharmonic Hall.
■ Rooms at the Hope Street Hotel start at £103, hopestreethotel.co.uk

HISTORIC YORK

It's a joy to wander medieval York's narrow streets in autumn – Halloween is a particularly great time for haunted tours. Be sure to take a photo in The Shambles, a narrow cobbled lane lined with 15th century Tudor buildings. Indoors, head for York Minster, the largest medieval cathedral in northern Europe and, for a bit of fun, get involved at the Jorvik Viking Centre, an interactive reconstruction of a Viking settlement. You don't need to be a trainspotter to be impressed by the National Railway Museum. Hungry? Head to Guy Fawkes Inn (his birthplace).
■ Rooms at the Georgian House & Mews start at £80, georgian house.co.uk

EXETER

This Devon city has traces of Roman times, plus medieval and Georgian buildings, cobbled streets and a Gothic cathedral. The quayside is home to former warehouses that have been converted into artsy boutiques and cafés. Want to get active? Walk along the quay, cycle, hire a canoe or kayak, or take a boat trip. Exeter is also filled with green spaces, home to plentiful wildlife, and many are linked by the 12-mile Exeter Green Circle walking trail.
■ Rooms at Leonardo Hotel start at £62, leonardo-hotels.com

Leafy Cambridge

The university city of Cambridge makes for a relaxed weekend away. The college buildings dominate, from the Gothic King's College Chapel to the Tudor elegance of Trinity College. But there's also the Fitzwilliam Museum, home to a vast collection of art and antiquities, and the Botanic Garden. Autumn is a great time to appreciate the tranquil riverside. The Backs – a series of gardens and parks behind the colleges – are best seen on water, whether you fancy punting yourself or taking a tour. Warm up with a hot chocolate from Jack's Gelato.
■ Rooms at the luxurious apartment-style The Fellows House start at £171, hilton.com

Perfectly plump

These super sweet pumpkins are made using a simple sock

All materials available from Hobbycraft.co.uk

You will need..

Socks	A glue gun
Scissors	Foraged twigs
A needle	Soft toy filling
Thread	Grey sheet of felt

1 Cut a sock in half at the heel and cut off the toe. Each sock will make two pumpkins.

2 Take one piece of the sock and turn it inside out. With a needle and thread, sew a running stitch around one of the open ends (leave a 1.5cm seam allowance).

3 Pull the thread to gather the fabric together and close the gap. Once it is pulled tightly, secure the thread with a couple of stitches.

4 Turn the sock back the correct way and you'll notice you now have a little pocket.

5 Fill the sock pocket with some polyester filling. Tip: to make your pumpkins different sizes, add more filling to some than others.

6 Sew the pumpkin closed. Use the same running stitch to gather the top of the sock together.

7 When the gap is closed, tuck the gathered seam allowance inside. Secure tightly with a few stitches.

8 Thread a doll needle with some yarn and tie a double knot at one end.

9 Bring the needle and yarn up through the centre of the pumpkin.

10 Wrap the yarn around the side of the pumpkin and thread the needle back up through the centre. Pull tightly to create the grooved effect.

11 Repeat this until you have six sections and tie off the yarn to secure.

12 Using a glue gun, attach a small foraged twig to the centre of the pumpkin. You can also glue on some foraged or felt leaves to finish.

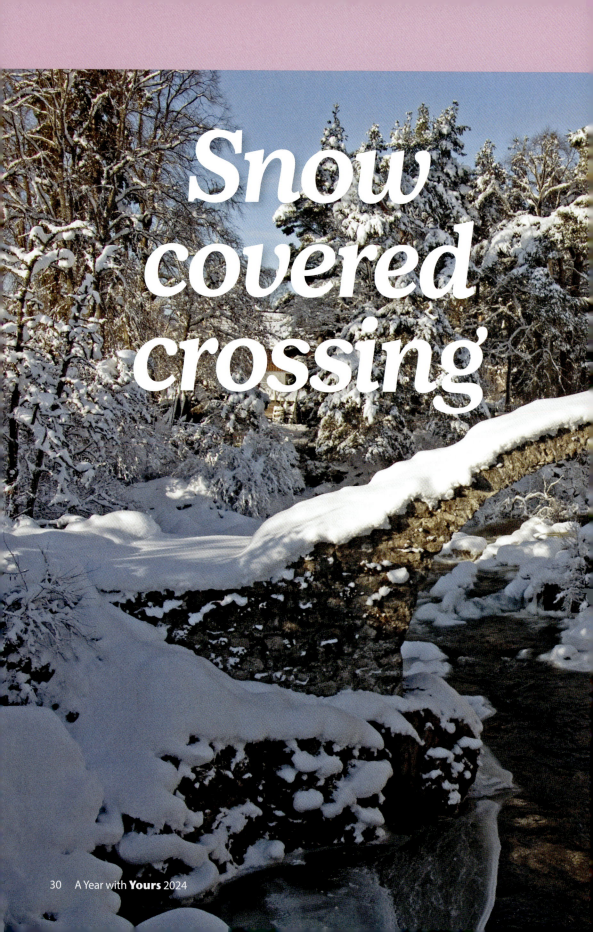

Snow covered crossing

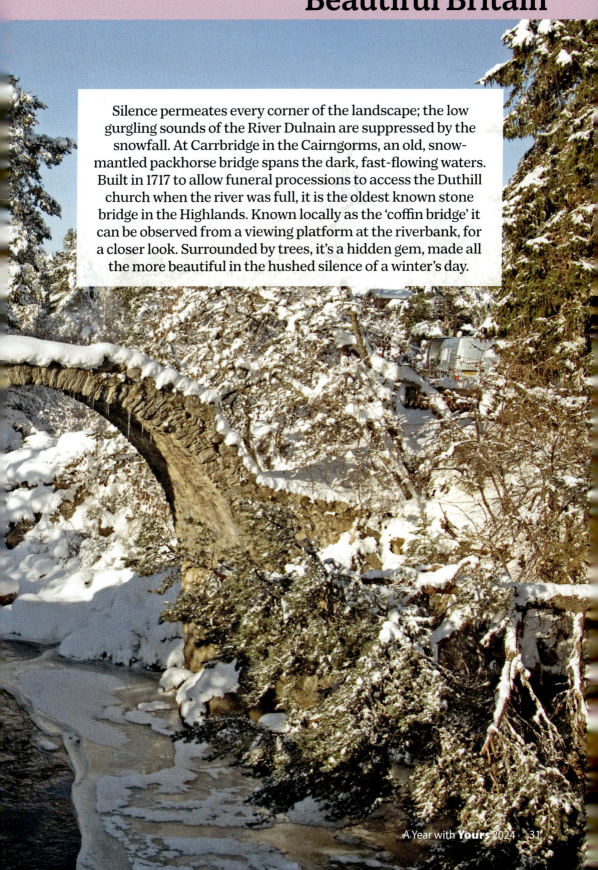

Beautiful Britain

Silence permeates every corner of the landscape; the low gurgling sounds of the River Dulnain are suppressed by the snowfall. At Carrbridge in the Cairngorms, an old, snow-mantled packhorse bridge spans the dark, fast-flowing waters. Built in 1717 to allow funeral processions to access the Duthill church when the river was full, it is the oldest known stone bridge in the Highlands. Known locally as the 'coffin bridge' it can be observed from a viewing platform at the riverbank, for a closer look. Surrounded by trees, it's a hidden gem, made all the more beautiful in the hushed silence of a winter's day.

Garden jobs

Simple steps to keep your plot looking good this season

Pause awhile and listen...

...to the winter song of robins, one of the only garden birds to continue singing through winter. Sweet and melancholy, it's the perfect tonic for shorter days.

TREAT YOURSELF AT THE GARDEN CENTRE

A few small pots of gorgeous winter favourites will transform your patio ready for festive guests. Scatter them about for a colourful surprise wherever visitors wander, or group a few pots together for a merry tabletop display.

SHOW YOUR SOIL SOME LOVE

Once your herbaceous plants – those with green stems rather than woody – have died back, add a layer of well-rotted compost, composted bark or leaf mould to the bare soil. This is great for your garden and the planet as healthy soil soaks up greenhouse gas carbon dioxide. As well as adding nutrients to the soil, it will stop heavy winter rain and strong winds washing or blowing it away.

Winter gardening

De-ice ponds

Surface ice can cause toxic gasses from the breakdown of dead leaves to build up and stop new oxygen getting into the water. Fill a plastic bowl with hot water and hold it over the ice to melt a hole and allow oxygen in. To stop it icing over again, float a tennis ball in the water.

RECYCLE YOUR TREE

If your Christmas tree has roots, plant it in your garden now. Dig a hole, plunge it in, still in its pot. Fill the hole with soil, keep it well hydrated and feed in spring (try Empathy After Plant Evergreen, £7.99/1L, amazon.co.uk).

GROW A BUFFET FOR EARLY BEES

A feast for the eyes and pollen lovers, crocuses are the jewels of the winter garden with their brightly coloured flowers in shades of purple, white and gold. On a sunny day, the goblet shaped blooms open out to a near flat star shape, allowing pollinating insects to get to the precious nectar within. Look for trays of them in garden centres that have plenty of buds but are not yet in bloom, and plant them in a sunny spot.

PILE UP YOUR PRUNINGS

A big mound of sticks makes a welcome nesting site for wrens and dunnocks – just make sure it's enough of a tangle that cats, magpies and other predators can't get into it too.

SPRUCE UP WOOD

Fencing and trellis will be easier to get to now plants are leaf-free, so choose a dry spell to give it a coat of preservative. Remember that drying will take longer in cool temperatures.

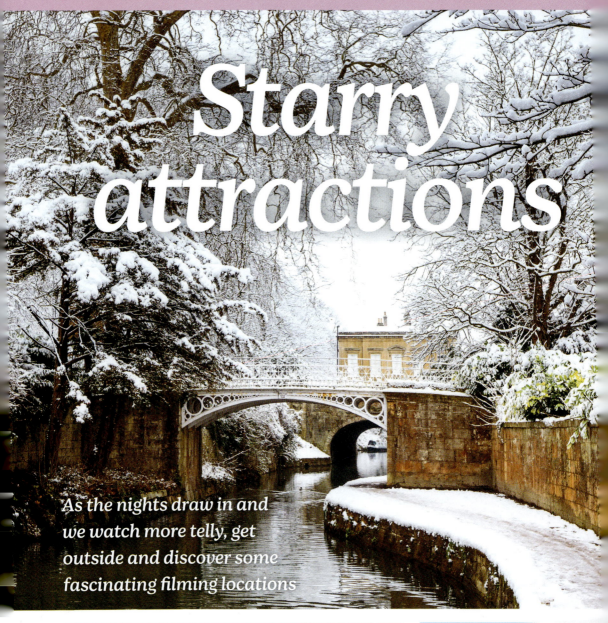

Starry attractions

As the nights draw in and we watch more telly, get outside and discover some fascinating filming locations

BRIDGERTON AND QUEEN CHARLOTTE, BATH

It's not surprising Netflix decided to come to Bath to film much of its entertaining period drama Bridgerton and the prequel Queen Charlotte: A Bridgerton Story – this small city has conserved much of its Georgian-era appearance. During the summer months, crowds of tourists can stop you from imagining yourself back in Regency times, whereas in winter you'll be able to photograph the Grade I listed The Crescent. Many of the outdoor shots of Bridgerton were filmed in Bath, and the National Trust's Bath Assembly Rooms and the Holburne Museum were used to create Lady Danbury's house.

■ Find a self-guided walking tour at beautifulbath.co.uk

DOC MARTIN, CORNWALL

Doc Martin may have finished, but after ten series, our love for this popular drama series never wanes. The fictional Cornish seaside village of Portwenn was actually Port Isaac, a small and picturesque fishing village in north Cornwall. You can wander around the village on your own, but Britmovie's 1.5-hour fully guided walking tour will bring more colour to your visit. The walking tour is led by a local who worked as an extra on Doc Martin and who is happy to share an anecdote or two! You'll visit locations including the Doc's house and surgery, Louisa's school and Mrs Tishell's pharmacy. Beyond the show, you'll get to discover the history of the village and its historic buildings and have time to admire beautiful views.
■ **Tour costs £15 for adults, see britmovietours.com**

The Crown, Scotland

It's no wonder Scotland features so predominantly in The Crown – the Royal family have enjoyed a long love affair with the country. Series six showcased St Andrew's – where William first met Kate while the pair were studying at the university – and you can take a guided walking tour of the town to get familiar with its highlights. Ardverikie House in Kinloch Laggan also stood in for Balmoral Castle (it also starred in Monarch of the Glen). You can explore the estate at any time and enjoy the Highland scenery, plus there are self-catering cottages to stay in.
■ **Walking tour of St Andrews £12, see walkingtoursin.com**

THE REPAIR SHOP, CHICHESTER

The Repair Shop has a unique mix of nostalgia, inspiring craftsmanship and life-affirming stories – who hasn't welled up when upholsterer Jay Blades and his team of restoration experts have brought back life to a cherished family heirloom? The show is filmed in the Court Barn at the Weald & Downland Living Museum in West Sussex. During filming, the area around the barn is closed to the public, but on selected dates you can look at the production set.
■ **Adults £15.50, see wealddown.co.uk/the-repair-shop/**

Call the Midwife, Kent

The start of a new year usually means a new series of Call the Midwife to look forward to! The long-running series about the lives of a group of midwives from the 1950s onwards is set in Poplar, East London, but the filming takes place at The Historic Dockyard Chatham. A guided tour, led by a costumed midwife, takes in familiar 'Poplar' building plus locations such as Chummy's Hill, where Nurse Noakes learnt to ride her bike (who can forget it!). You can also see an exhibition of props. Organise a tour directly or why not make it part of a longer break? Coracle Coaches runs a fully guided tour, plus a two-night, half-board stay at the Orida Hotel, and excursions to Windsor and Canterbury (including coach travel). Perfect if your other half isn't such a Call the Midwife devotee!
■ **Adults £27, see thedockyard.co.uk. Coracle two-night trip and tour from £269, coraclecoaches.co.uk**

A touch of magic

Get children squealing with excitement with this lovely handmade Christmas Eve activity box

Seasonal crafts

All materials available from Hobbycraft.co.uk

You will need...

For the box:
Wooden storage box
30 x 20cm
Red and gold paint
Black and gold card
Glue

For the sweetie tree decorations:
Air dry clay
A straw
A rolling pin
A round cutter/cup
Green and red paint
Clay varnish
Red double-faced ribbon

For the Santa plate:
Paper plate
Felt tip pens

For the reindeer food:
A brown envelope
Foam reindeer head
Red pom poms
Porridge oats

Reindeer hot chocolate:
Plastic cone bag
Hot chocolate powder
Mini white marshmallows
Googly eyes
Glue
Red pom pom
Brown and festive coloured pipe cleaners

Santa milk bottle:
Glass bottle
Red and white pom poms
Glue

Sweetie tree decorations

1 Roll out some air dry clay to a thickness of about 1cm. Use a cookie cutter (ours was about 8cm diameter) to cut out two circles. Make a hole near the edge using a straw and leave to dry overnight.

2 Draw festive swirls on the clay with pencil then paint green and red. Leave to dry, then paint a personalised message to Santa on the back.

3 Once dry, add a coat of varnish for durability and a shine. Thread through a length of red ribbon for hanging.

The box

1 Paint the box red on the outside and gold on the inside.

2 For the belt, cut a 5cm wide strip of black card and glue it across the centre of the lid. Cut 4 more 5cm strips to fit the sides of the lid and box and glue in place to look like the belt wraps around the box. For the buckle, draw a 5cm square with a 2.5cm border onto gold card and glue onto the centre of the belt.

Reindeer hot chocolate

1 Fill three quarters of the cone bag with hot chocolate. Pop white marshmallows on top and seal shut with Sellotape.

2 Use strong glue to glue on the googly eyes and a red pom pom nose. Bend pipe cleaners into the shape of antlers and tape onto the back of the reindeer's head. Glue a stripey pipe cleaner around the top of the bag to conceal.

Santa milk bottle

Use strong glue to stick 6 red pom poms onto the front of the glass bottle to make a Santa hat. Take the white pom poms and glue 1 to the top and 4 along the bottom of the hat.

Reindeer food

Glue a reindeer foam shape onto the front of the envelope, then glue on a red pom pom for Rudolph's nose. Pour 2 or 3 tablespoons of porridge oats into the brown envelope and seal with tape.

Santa plate

Use a pencil to mark out an outline of a carrot, mince pie and glass of milk. Write a Christmas message and add semi-circles around the rim. Use markers to go over the pencil and add lots of colour.

Notable dates 2024

New Year's Day (Bank Holiday observed)	Monday January 1
Bank Holiday (Scotland)	Tuesday January 2
Epiphany	Saturday January 6
Burns Night	Thursday January 25
Chinese New Year (Dragon)	Saturday February 10
Shrove Tuesday (Pancake Day)	Tuesday February 13
Valentine's Day	Wednesday February 14
Ash Wednesday	Wednesday February 14
St David's Day	Friday March 1
Mothering Sunday	Sunday March 10
First Day of Ramadan (Islam)	Sunday March 10
St Patrick's Day Bank Holiday (N. Ireland/Eire)	Monday March 18
Palm Sunday	Sunday March 24
Maundy Thursday	Thursday March 28
Good Friday (Bank Holiday)	Friday March 29
Easter Sunday	Sunday March 31
Easter Monday (Bank Holiday)	Monday April 1
First Day of Passover (Jewish Holiday)	Monday April 22
St George's Day	Tuesday April 23
May Day (Early May Bank Holiday)	Monday May 6
Ascension Day	Thursday May 9
Spring Bank Holiday	Monday May 27
Father's Day	Sunday June 16
Summer Solstice (Longest Day)	Thursday June 20
Armed Forces Day	Saturday June 29
American Independence Day	Thursday July 4
Islamic New Year	Saturday July 6
Battle of the Boyne (Holiday N. Ireland)	Friday July 12
St Swithin's Day	Monday July 15
Summer Bank Holiday (Scotland/Eire)	Monday August 5
Summer Bank Holiday	Monday August 26
Jewish New Year (Rosh Hashanah)	Thursday October 3
Trafalgar Day	Monday October 21
Diwali (Hindu Festival)	Thursday October 31
Hallowe'en	Thursday October 31
All Saints' Day	Friday November 1
Guy Fawkes Night	Tuesday November 5
Remembrance Sunday	Sunday November 10
St Andrew's Day	Saturday November 30
First Sunday in Advent	Sunday December 1
Winter Solstice (Shortest Day)	Saturday December 21
Christmas Day	Wednesday December 25
Boxing Day	Thursday December 26
New Year's Eve/Hogmanay	Tuesday December 31

THE YEAR AHEAD

31 SUNDAY

1 MONDAY

2 TUESDAY

3 WEDNESDAY

4 THURSDAY

5 FRIDAY

6 SATURDAY

On this week...

January 2nd 1972

ANYONE FOR TENNIS?

English tennis player Virginia Wade stormed to victory in the women's singles final of the 1972 Australian Open. It was second-seeded Virginia's first Grand Slam title, defeating Aussie favourite Evonne Goolagong on her home turf 6-4, 6-4.

During her career, Virginia won three major singles championships and four doubles titles and is the only British woman in history to have won titles at all four majors. Her most famous success was winning Wimbledon in 1977, the tournament's centenary year, as well as the year of the Silver Jubilee of Queen Elizabeth II, who attended Wimbledon for the first time since 1962 to watch the final.

Over her 26-year career, Wade won 55 professional singles championships and amassed $1,542,278 in prize money. She was ranked in the world's top 10 continuously between 1967 and 1979.

After retiring from singles competitions at the end of 1985, Wade became a sports commentator for the BBC.

Fun anagram!
Change agree into another word for keen

Answer: Eager

Money-saving tip

Have a 'one in, one out' rule – so before you buy something new in the sales, sell something else first. The same goes for subscriptions. If you sign up to something new, ask yourself what you can remove. Can you share subscriptions with friends to lower costs too?

Mood boosters

Nature offers an instant pick-me-up, so why not vow to explore further than your local park this year by visiting one of the UK's incredible National Parks, protected because of their beautiful countryside. Visit Dartmoor's ponies, see the towering Cairngorms, or wander along Hadrian's Wall. See nationalparks.uk

A PHOTO TO TREASURE

This photo is of me with my mother. She was widely travelled and observed many traditions including 'first footing' on New Year's Eve. Aged four, I was very excited to be allowed to stay up until past midnight to experience the fun with the adults.
Charmaine Fletcher, via email

Recipe of the week

HASSELBACK SQUASH WITH WALNUT CRUMB

SERVES: **2** PREP: **15 mins** COOK: **1 hour**

1 butternut squash, peeled, halved and de-seeded
2 cloves garlic, sliced
3 tbsp olive oil, plus a drizzle
2 tsp ground cumin
1 tsp ground coriander
75g (3oz) California Walnuts, chopped, plus 25g (1oz)
½ x 25g (1oz) pack fresh coriander, chopped, plus extra to serve
2 tbsp chopped chives
1 lemon
150g (5oz) edamame beans

1. Preheat the oven to 200C/180C Fan/Gas Mark 6.
2. Place one squash half, flat side down, on a chopping board between two wooden spoons (to stop the knife cutting all the way through). Make cuts, 0.5cm apart, all the way along the squash. Repeat with the other squash half and place both in a roasting tin. Push the garlic slices randomly into the cuts.
3. Mix 2 tbsp oil with the spices and drizzle over the squash, bake for 40 mins.
4. Mix the 75g (3oz) walnuts, herbs, lemon zest and remaining oil together and sprinkle over the squash, bake for a further 20 mins until golden and tender.
5. Meanwhile, stir-fry the beans and remaining 25g (1oz) walnuts in a drizzle of oil for 1-2 mins, stirring in the juice of half the lemon at the end. Serve with the squash.

CALIFORNIA WALNUTS

7 SUNDAY

8 MONDAY

9 TUESDAY

10 WEDNESDAY

11 THURSDAY

12 FRIDAY

13 SATURDAY

On this week...

January 10th 1982

FROZEN BRITAIN

A severe cold front blanketed much of the country, and the UK recorded its lowest ever temperature of -27.2°C at Braemar in Aberdeenshire, equalling the record set in the same place in 1895. It was a record that wouldn't be equalled until 1995.

Lengthy queues formed on city streets for bread and milk, soldiers were even drafted in to dig families out of their homes and helicopters scrambled to transport food to remote farms.

In some parts of Wales it snowed solidly for 36 hours, leaving entire front doors submerged and cars buried. The snow was 60cm deep, though drifts reportedly reached up to six metres high. This photo shows one gentleman in Bedlinog, between Pontypridd and Merthyr, standing in a 'tunnel' dug through the snow so that he could reach his front door

Fun anagram!

Change **thicken** into a place where you cook

Answer: Kitchen

Money-saving tip

Make sure your credit score is as good as it can be – so that you benefit from lower interest rates on loans and credit cards, and therefore save money – by paying your bills on time and checking you're on the electoral register (it's easy to slip off – check at gov.uk).

Mood boosters

Meditating, even for short periods of time, has been proven to reduce pain, lower blood pressure, reduce stress and release happy chemicals in the brain – serotonin, dopamine and endorphins – all of which work together to put you in a better mood. Give it a go!

A PHOTO TO TREASURE

All my life I dreamed of visiting the Potala Palace in Tibet. As the photo shows, I was finally able to fulfil my ambition at the age of 50. It just goes to prove that you should never give up on your hopes and dreams.

Lorraine Smith, via email

Recipe of the week

SWEET POTATO WAFFLES

SERVES: **4** PREP: **50 mins** COOK: **20 mins**

1 large sweet potato
300ml (10fl oz) almond milk
1 tbsp apple cider vinegar
3 tbsp olive oil, plus extra for cooking
180g (6oz) gluten-free plain flour
1½ tsp baking powder
¾ tsp sweet smoked paprika
2 spring onions, finely sliced
Small bunch dill and parsley, finely chopped
Sea salt and freshly ground black pepper
For the spinach:
2 tablespoons olive oil
400g (14oz) frozen spinach, defrosted and drained
¼ tsp grated nutmeg
1 tbsp dairy-free butter
Sea salt and freshly ground black pepper
Dairy-free crème fraîche, sour cream or yogurt, to serve

1. Preheat the oven to 220C/200C Fan/Gas Mark 7. Bake the sweet potato for 40-45 mins. Let cool, then scoop out the flesh. Place in a bowl to one side.
2. Pour the milk into a jug and stir in the vinegar. Leave to one side for 5 mins, then stir in 3 tbsp of olive oil.
3. Sift the flour, baking powder and smoked paprika into a large bowl. Stir through the chopped herbs. Make a well in the flour mix and pour in the milk mixture.
4. Mash the sweet potato flesh, add to the batter and whisk.
5. Preheat a waffle maker and brush with oil. Pour the batter into the waffle maker and cook for 6 mins. Keep warm while you repeat with the remaining batter.
6. While the waffles are cooking, prepare the spinach. Add the oil to a pan and place over a medium heat. When glossy, add the spinach and cook gently.
7. Add in the nutmeg and dairy-free butter and season. Serve alongside the waffles with a few dollops of dairy-free crème fraîche, sour cream or yogurt.

SEASONAL SPUDS

14 SUNDAY

15 MONDAY

16 TUESDAY

17 WEDNESDAY

18 THURSDAY

19 FRIDAY

20 SATURDAY

On this week...

January 16th 1952

IZZY WHIZZY, LET'S GET BUSY!

The UK's most famous glove puppet bear, Sooty, first appeared on TV as part of the BBC's Talent Night. Sooty had been discovered by magician and puppeteer Harry Corbett a few years earlier in a joke shop on Blackpool's North Pier. After paying 7s/6d for the original yellow bear glove puppet, then called Teddy, he began entertaining his children, David and Peter.

Following Sooty's debut he was offered a part in Peter Butterworth's show Saturday Special. He was such a hit the BBC offered Harry and his puppet pal their own six-episode series, combining simple magic and slapstick comedy.

Although his human companion has changed over the years, Sooty remains popular to this day and, in 2016, the show was entered into the Guinness Book of Records as the longest-running children's TV programme in the world.

In 1976 Harry Corbett and Sooty were both awarded OBEs for charitable services.

Money-saving tip

Don't rinse or soak plates before putting them in the dishwasher – dishwasher programs include a rinse at the start, so you'll effectively be paying twice for the hot water. Stack larger plates at the back so they don't interrupt the flow of water and prevent other items from cleaning properly.

Mood boosters

Don't save things for "best" – you're missing out on the joy they can bring. Consider every day a special occasion – wear your best outfit to the shops, open that fancy bottle you were given as a gift on a Monday and wear your most special piece of jewellery to the library!

A PHOTO TO TREASURE

This photo was taken just before my son was born in 1978. Decorating his bedroom was our first attempt at DIY and the expensive Paddington Bear wallpaper was a nightmare to put up. We were one strip short and had to buy a whole new roll to finish the job.

Yvette Loader, via email

Recipe of the week

COFFEE, CARAMEL AND PECAN LAYER CAKE

SERVES: **10** PREP: **15 mins** COOK: **25 mins**

370g (13oz) unsalted butter, split 250g (9oz) and 120g (4oz)
400g (14oz) caster sugar, split 250g (9oz) and 150g (5oz)
4 eggs
250g (9oz) self-raising flour
1 tsp baking powder
3 fresh espressos (120ml/4fl oz) or 1 tbsp + 1 tsp instant coffee dissolved in 5 tbsp of boiling water
150g (5oz) pecans, roughly chopped + extra for decorating
150ml (2fl oz) double cream
1 tsp salt
500g (18oz) icing sugar

1. Preheat your oven to 180C/160C Fan/Gas Mark 4 and line your cake tins with baking parchment.
2. To make the sponge, cream together 250g (9oz) of butter and 250g (9oz) of caster sugar, then add the eggs.
3. Add in the flour and baking powder, two of the espressos, and mix.
4. Stir in pecans and divide between three 8in cake tins.
5. Bake for 20-25 mins until golden. Leave to cool.
6. Make the caramel by heating the remaining 150g (5oz) of caster sugar and 5fl oz of water in a saucepan over a medium-high heat until boiling, without stirring.
7. Once the caramel is amber (around 5 mins) pour in the cream, stirring continuously. Once combined, stir in the salt and transfer the caramel to a bowl to cool.
8. To make the buttercream combine the remaining 120g (4oz) butter, icing sugar and the final espresso in the bowl and cream together until smooth.
9. Save 60g (2oz) caramel for the drip, then assemble the cake by sandwiching each layer with the buttercream and a spoonful of caramel spread on top before lightly coating the top and sides with buttercream.
10. Sprinkle on chopped and whole pecans and serve.

EASY PEASY BAKING CAMPAIGN

21 SUNDAY

22 MONDAY

23 TUESDAY

24 WEDNESDAY

25 THURSDAY

26 FRIDAY

27 SATURDAY

On this week...

January 26th 1973

SWEET SUCCESS!

Glam rock band The Sweet secured their first UK No.1 with their single Blockbuster! The London band, featuring singer Brian Connolly, bassist Steve Priest, guitarist Andy Scott and drummer Mick Tucker, had their first hit in 1971 with Funny Funny.

The chart-topping success of Blockbuster! paved the way for 13 Top 20 hits in the Seventies, including Hell Raiser, The Ballroom Blitz and Teenage Rampage.

To promote their singles, Sweet made several TV appearances on Top of the Pops. Outrageous stage costumes were an integral part of the glam rock culture. After one performance of Blockbuster! there were complaints because Priest performed dressed in German military uniform, Hitler moustache and swastika armband.

Their last successful single was Love Is Like Oxygen in 1978. Connolly left the group the following year to start a solo career and the remaining members disbanded in 1981.

Fun anagram!
Change cheater into a job

Answer: Teacher

Money-saving tip

Keep your car tyres pumped up! Under-inflated tyres cause a vehicle to use up to 10 per cent more fuel. As the average petrol tank is 42 litres and the average household uses one tank a month, driving with under-inflated tyres could cost an extra £7.50 a month.

Mood boosters

Helping others is a win-win mood booster, and it doesn't have to cost you a penny. A Swiss study found that volunteering gave the helpers a higher life satisfaction. Apparently, two hours a week is the optimal time to dedicate to others in order to enrich your life and be happier.

A PHOTO TO TREASURE

This is one of my favourite photographs. I had the time of my life when I was lucky enough to meet up with the owner of these beautiful mountain dogs and spent a wonderful time with them in the Himalayas.

Gordon Smith, via email

Recipe of the week

VEGGIE SAUSAGE AND BEAN PIE

SERVES: **4** PREP: **10 mins** COOK: **20 mins**

2 x packets Idahoan Cheddar Cheese Perfect Mash
1 pack veggie sausages
Sunflower oil
1 onion, diced
415g (15oz) can of baked beans
4 tbsp tomato ketchup
75g (3oz) cheddar cheese
Steamed green vegetables, to serve

1. Preheat the oven to 190C/375F/Gas Mark 5.
2. Make the Idahoan Cheddar Cheese Perfect Mash according to the instructions.
3. Fry the sausages in the oil for 2-3 mins until golden on the outside, remove from the pan and set aside.
4. Add the onion and cook until softened, approximately 5 mins. Add beans, ketchup and 80ml of water and simmer for 3-4 mins. Stir in the sausages.
5. Place the mixture into an ovenproof dish, top with the mashed potato and sprinkle with the grated cheese, then bake in a pre-heated oven for 20 mins.
6. Serve with steamed green vegetables.

IDAHOAN PERFECT MASH

28 SUNDAY

29 MONDAY

30 TUESDAY

31 WEDNESDAY

1 THURSDAY

2 FRIDAY

3 SATURDAY

On this week...

February 2nd 1952

FANCY FRENCH DESIGNS

Fashion designer Hubert de Givenchy presented his first collection in Paris and left an indelible mark on history.

Aged just 25, Givenchy had decided to take a huge risk and branch out on his own. With a shoestring staff and cramped space, he was able to undercut other couture houses by a third. But it was his designs, not his prices, that earned him the biggest ovation and sales of seven million francs ($20,000) on the first day.

Givenchy became famous for his love of les séparables (separates). Elegant blouses and floaty skirts, blending architectural lines and simplicity, was a contrast to the more constricted looks of the day. His friend and public relations expert Bettina Graziani opened the show, wearing what would become famous as the 'Bettina blouse'.

Givenchy soon caught the attention of Hollywood starlet Audrey Hepburn and the pair became close friends, with him dressing her for films such as Sabrina, Breakfast at Tiffany's and Charade.

Fun anagram!

Change asleep into a word used by polite people

Answer: Please

Money-saving tip

Buy laundry detergent in bulk to save money. The average adult does 208 washes per year – if you buy a 130-wash bottle of detergent for £15, it will cost you £30 per year or 11p per wash. A regular 35-wash bottle of detergent will cost you £35 per year or 16p per wash.

Mood boosters

Your body holds on to stress. Before doing anything that makes you anxious, stretch your arms and legs, as a couple of minutes stretching can help you relax. It's common to hold your breath and tense your muscles when stressed – this freeze response holds fear in your body, so walk around to loosen it.

A PHOTO TO TREASURE

This is me with my best friend Angela at her 80th birthday party. She is on the left, holding the flowers. We have been firm friends ever since I was widowed over ten years ago and moved into the house across the road from hers.

Angela Patchett, via email

Recipe of the week

RED PESTO AND PARMESAN DOUGH TWISTS

MAKES: **8** PREP: **25 mins** COOK: **20 mins**

1 packet fast action yeast
220ml (7fl oz) warm water
200g (7oz) wholemeal flour
200g (7oz) plain flour
1 tbsp white sugar
1 tsp salt
½ jar red pesto (more for dipping)
75g (3oz) chopped walnuts
170g (6oz) parmesan cheese

1. Preheat the oven to 200C/180C Fan/Gas Mark 6.
2. In a measuring jug, combine the warm water and yeast. Stir and set to one side for 2-3 mins to activate the yeast.
3. In a large mixing bowl, combine the flours, sugar and salt. Pour in the yeast and water and stir them together with your hand to form a dough.
4. Sprinkle your worktop with a little flour and knead the dough until smooth, then return to the large mixing bowl, cover and leave in a warm place for at least 15 mins to prove (this is where it will start to grow in size).
5. Using your fist, knock the dough back (this means push the dough back down to its original size) and tip out onto a floured work surface before rolling into a large rectangle shape (about 5mm thickness).
6. Spread the red pesto on half of the rectangle, sprinkle over the walnuts, grate a thin layer of cheese on top and then fold half of the dough over the pesto and parmesan.
7. Cut the dough into 1-inch wide strips, then, holding each end, twist each one before placing onto a lined baking tray.
8. Bake for 15-20 mins until risen and golden, then remove from the oven, allow to cool slightly, grate more cheese on top and serve.

BARI THE DIETITIAN

4 SUNDAY

5 MONDAY

6 TUESDAY

7 WEDNESDAY

8 THURSDAY

9 FRIDAY

10 SATURDAY

On this week...

February 4th 1983

RAISE A GLASS!

American sitcom Cheers made its UK debut on Channel 4. Ted Danson played Sam Malone, the owner of a Boston bar where a group of misfit locals meet to drink and socialise.

The cast included aggressively intolerant Carla (Rhea Perlman), jilted waitress Diane (Shelley Long), Sam's ex-coach Ernie (Nicholas Colasanto) and barfly Norm (George Wendt). The show was a phenomenal success with 275 episodes over 11 seasons.

One of the regulars at the bar also sparked off another hugely successful comedy. Dr Frasier Crane, played by Kelsey Grammer, a haughty, insecure psychiatrist and his frosty psychologist wife Dr Lilith Sternin were the inspiration for the Seattle-based comedy Frasier. Many of the Cheers cast members had cameos in the show, which is said to be one of the most successful TV spin-offs.

Fun anagram!
Change beard into something you eat

Answer: Bread

Money-saving tip

Don't buy new household items before checking if you can borrow them first. Food-sharing app Olio has a Borrow function so users can list commonly used household items that are available for their neighbours to borrow temporarily – everything from power tools to pasta makers!

Mood boosters

From planting wildflower meadows to preserving our woodlands, or even looking after otters, volunteering outdoors is a great way to connect with our natural world, plus learn new skills. For opportunities see Wildlifetrusts.org, Tcv.org.uk, Woodlandtrust.org.uk and Nationaltrust.org.uk.

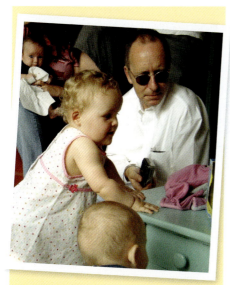

A PHOTO TO TREASURE

Here is my daughter Emily on her first birthday with her Granddad Rob, Nana Viv and baby cousin Daniel. I love her expression – she still has that same sense of wonder and curiosity now that she is 20 and a student at the University of York.

Sam Hendley, via email

Recipe of the week

BEER BATTERED CHIPS WITH SPECIAL CURRY

SERVES: **2** PREP: **15 mins** COOK: **15 mins**

1 pack of Mash Direct Beer Battered Chips
1 tsp oil
1 onion, finely chopped
2 chicken breast fillets, trimmed and cut into bite size pieces
400ml (14fl oz) coconut milk
1 chicken stock cube, crumbled
2 garlic cloves, crushed
1 tsp grated fresh ginger
3 tbsp medium curry powder
50g (2oz) tomato puree
45g (2oz) mango chutney
The juice of 1 lime
200g (7oz) prawns (optional)
200g (7oz) frozen peas
2 spring onions, finely chopped
A handful of chopped coriander

1. Cook the Mash Direct Beer Battered Chips as per packet instructions.
2. Heat the oil in a large saucepan and fry the onion until soft. Add the chicken pieces and fry for 3-4 mins. Remove to a plate and keep warm.
3. Add the coconut milk, stock cube, garlic, ginger, curry powder, tomato puree, mango chutney and lime juice to the saucepan and boil. Reduce the temperature to simmer for 5-10 mins until the sauce thickens.
4. Return the chicken to the pan and cook for a few minutes. Add the prawns, peas and warm through.
5. Arrange the Beer Battered Chips onto warm bowls and top with special curry.
6. Scatter with spring onions and coriander.

MASH DIRECT

11 SUNDAY

12 MONDAY

13 TUESDAY

14 WEDNESDAY

15 THURSDAY

16 FRIDAY

17 SATURDAY

On this week...

February 15th 1952

KING GEORGE VI'S FUNERAL

King George VI was laid to rest at St George's Chapel on his Windsor Castle estate. The King passed away in his sleep at the age of 56 after 16 years on the throne.

The King's body had lain in state for three days at Westminster Hall, where more than 300,000 people attended to pay homage. From here the cortège, made up of foreign royalty, heads of state and the armed forces, began its dignified progress through London.

Dressed in black, the Princess Royal, Princess Margaret, the new Queen Elizabeth and the Queen Mother were in the first carriage. They were followed on foot by the Dukes of Edinburgh, Gloucester and Windsor in dress uniform and the young Duke of Kent in formal mourning wear.

Crowds gathered in the early hours of the morning to watch the solemn procession through the capital's streets. Thousands more people were also able to witness the event on television.

Fun anagram!

Change **below** into a part of the body

Answer: Bowel or elbow

Money-saving tip

When shopping online, put the items you want in your basket, then wait for 24 hours. Often you'll be sent a discount code as an incentive to purchase (clear your browsing history so the store thinks you're a new customer too).

Mood boosters

Studies have shown that eating soon after you wake can help to balance your blood sugar and hormone levels, to give you vitality and mental focus for the day ahead. There's also a psychological effect of having a good breakfast – you'll know you've taken the right steps from the outset!

A PHOTO TO TREASURE

This photo is of me hugging my granddad, Sid, on my wedding day. Sid was a true gentleman, adored by his family and anyone who met him. He loved to travel abroad as well as tending his veggie patch where he grew the tastiest carrots, potatoes and green beans.

Kerry Barnard, via email

Recipe of the week

KINDER BUENO BROWNIES

SERVES: **16** PREP: **10 mins** COOK: **30 mins**

135g (5oz) unsalted butter
150g (5oz) dark chocolate, broken into pieces + 50g (2oz) for drizzling
350g (12oz) light brown sugar
3 eggs
130g (5oz) plain flour
2 tbsp / 30g (1oz) cocoa powder
6 bars Kinder Bueno (12 fingers)

1. Preheat the oven to 180C/160C Fan/Gas Mark 4.
2. Put the butter and 150g (5oz) of dark chocolate in a large microwavable bowl and melt it in the microwave in 10 second intervals, being careful not to burn it.
3. Add in the sugar and combine with a wooden spoon or spatula before adding the eggs, followed by the flour and cocoa powder, stirring until there are no lumps.
4. Pour half of the brownie batter into a lined 20cm tin and spread evenly. Take four Kinder Bueno bars (eight fingers) and lay them on top of the batter.
5. Pour the remaining batter on top and spread to cover the Kinder Buenos.
6. Bake in a preheated oven for 20 mins, then remove, break up the remaining two Kinder Buenos into segments and push gently into the top of the brownie. Return the brownie to the oven for the last 10 mins.
7. Allow to cool completely before melting the remaining 50g (2oz) of dark chocolate, drizzling over the top and portioning into squares.

EASY PEASY BAKING CAMPAIGN

18 SUNDAY

19 MONDAY

20 TUESDAY

21 WEDNESDAY

22 THURSDAY

23 FRIDAY

24 SATURDAY

On this week...

February 18th 1998

MUSIC TO OUR EARS

Italian tenor Andrea Bocelli made his operatic debut as Rodolfo in La Bohème at the Teatro Lirico in Cagliari, having been 'discovered' by Luciano Pavarotti, who heard a demo tape of the young singer and suggested he tour with Italian rock star Zucchero.

Andrea has since sold more than 75 million records worldwide, becoming one of the best-loved performers of all time.

Indeed, the singer's reach is, quite literally, out of this world. In 2001, the first space tourist, Dennis Tito, asked to include one of Bocelli's albums in his 7kg baggage allowance when he spent eight days in orbit on a visit to the International Space Station.

Born with impaired vision as a result of congenital glaucoma, Andrea was blinded in a football accident at the age of 12, but music has always been his salvation. And, at the age of 66, the father of three shows no signs of retiring. His world tour continues in 2024, visit andreabocelli.com for dates.

Fun anagram!
Change chain into a country

Answer: China

Money-saving tip

When booking flights and holidays, do check travel agents as they have access to exclusive deals you won't be able to access privately. For hotels, call them directly to ask if they can match other deals online – very often they'll surprise you.

Mood boosters

We all know that exercise can boost your mood, but for the best effects get active in the morning. One study has shown that the mood-boosting effects of a simple walk or run in the park can last for up to seven hours.

A PHOTO TO TREASURE

This photo always makes me smile as it's a reminder of many happy Sunday lunches shared with my parents. Sadly, dementia took our dear dad from us in 2021 but photos like this one keep the memories of wonderful times alive in our hearts.

Sandra Evitt, via email

Recipe of the week

SUPER GREEN MATCHA PANCAKES

SERVES: **1** PREP: **10 mins** COOK: **15 mins**

130g (5oz) self-raising flour
1 tbsp caster sugar
1 tsp baking powder
1 tbsp matcha powder
Pinch of salt
2 tbsp unsalted butter, melted and cooled
2 medium British Lion eggs
100ml (3fl oz) whole milk
1 tsp green gel colouring (optional)
vegetable oil to fry
50ml double cream
20g (1oz) coconut yoghurt
20g (1oz) raspberries
Raspberry coulis, to serve (optional)

1. Start with making the pancake batter. In a medium size mixing bowl, combine all the dry ingredients: flour, sugar, baking powder, matcha powder and salt.
2. In a separate bowl mix together butter, eggs, milk and colouring (if using). Gradually pour the wet ingredients over the dry and whisk until the batter is smooth and there are no lumps of flour.
3. Warm up a teaspoon of oil in a small frying pan over a medium heat. When the oil is hot pour 2 tablespoons of batter into the centre of the pan and shape with the back of a spoon into a round disc. Cook for 2 mins on the first side, then flip and cook for another 2 mins until the pancake is golden brown. Transfer onto a cooling rack and cook the rest of the mixture.
4. In a small bowl, whip the double cream to a stiff peak consistency. Gently fold the yoghurt into the cream.
5. To serve, stack the pancakes, top them with coconut cream and fresh raspberries. Drizzle the raspberry coulis over the stack (if using).

BRITISH LION EGGS

25 SUNDAY

26 MONDAY

27 TUESDAY

28 WEDNESDAY

29 THURSDAY

1 FRIDAY

2 SATURDAY

On this week...

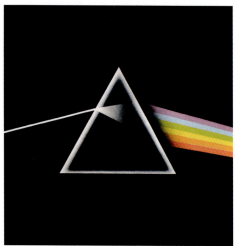

March 1st 1973

A CLASSIC ALBUM IS BORN

English rock band Pink Floyd released their eighth studio album, Dark Side of the Moon. The concept album, which includes the tracks Money and Us and Them, explores themes such as conflict, greed, time, death and mental illness. It has since become one of the most critically acclaimed albums of all time, with sales of more than 45 million.

This iconic album saw the London band leap the chasm between freewheeling psychedelic rock and global megalith, and still sounds incredible and relevant today.

Guitarist David Gilmour delivers one of his most expressive solos on Time. The song, about life's fleeting nature, also includes Roger Waters' classic line "Hanging on in quiet desperation is the English way".

Dark Side was very much bassist Roger's baby. He wrote or co-wrote the bulk of it and, 50 years on, his lyrics can be related to today's world. Satirical anthem Money ("Share it fairly but don't take a slice of my pie") certainly has a modern resonance.

Fun anagram!

Change carthorse into a group of musicians

Answer: Orchestra

Money-saving tip

For food bargains, consider buying in bulk and swerve the supermarkets – you may find better prices for sacks of rice or big bags of spices at your local Asian supermarket or specialist retailer. Go in with a friend so you can share the costs.

Mood boosters

Learn something new – exposing yourself to new ideas or activities, whether that's learning to salsa, joining a choir, reading a book you wouldn't usually choose, or playing a new sport – can be really invigorating. It's a great confidence-booster, and extensive research shows that it keeps your brain healthy, too.

A PHOTO TO TREASURE

This great photo was taken for the Cambridge Evening News when my band, Nutmeg, won a rock competition at the Cambridge Corn Exchange back in 1988. I am the guitarist seen in the background and the singer is my long-time friend Tom Dalpra.

Richard Scurrah, via email

Recipe of the week

MUSHROOM BOURGUIGNON

SERVES: **4** PREP: **15 mins** COOK: **1hr 15mins**

40ml (1fl oz) olive oil
½ leek, sliced
1 medium yellow onion or 2 shallots
3-4 minced or chopped garlic cloves
200g (7oz) diced carrots (fresh or frozen)
2 celery sticks, chopped (fresh or frozen)
3 tbsp tomato paste
2 tbsp all-purpose flour or potato starch
300ml (10fl oz) of (vegan) red wine
250ml (8fl oz) vegetable stock
50g (2oz) dried porcini mushrooms (soaked) or 200g (7oz) frozen (defrosted)
Sprigs of fresh thyme, parsley, rosemary
500g (18oz) fresh or 600g (21oz) frozen mushrooms, defrosted
80g (3oz) pearl onions (optional)
For garnish: chopped parsley and chives, or truffle oil

1. Preheat the oven to 160C/140C Fan/Gas Mark 3. In a pan, heat some of the olive oil over a medium heat.
2. Add the leek and onions and cook until slightly browned. Then add the garlic and set aside.
3. Using the same pan, increase the heat and add the rest of the oil. Sauté the carrots and celery, add the tomato paste and flour and cook for 2 mins.
4. Add the wine, cook for 3-4 mins, then add the stock and bring back to a boil. Add the mushrooms and herbs. Reduce the heat and simmer for 35-40 mins.
5. Using a slotted spoon, remove the vegetables and discard, reserving the wine sauce. Roughly chop the mushrooms and sauté. Add them to the wine sauce.
6. Peel and sauté the pearl onions in the same pan until lightly browned. Add the pearl onions to the mushroom mixture. Cover the pan, braise for 25-30 min. Top with chopped parsley, chives or truffle oil.

UK HEALTHY LIVING AND AGEING PLATFORM GOLDSTER

3 SUNDAY

4 MONDAY

5 TUESDAY

6 WEDNESDAY

7 THURSDAY

8 FRIDAY

9 SATURDAY

On this week...

March 7th 1962

THE BEATLES HIT THE AIR

The Playhouse Theatre in Manchester played host to The Beatles as they recorded their radio debut. The foursome – John Lennon, Paul McCartney, George Harrison and Pete Best – had been playing extensively in Hamburg, Germany but were still little known in the UK.

For their first live radio session they performed three cover versions: Dream Baby (How Long Must I Dream), Memphis Tennessee and Please Mister Postman. The show, Teenager's Turn – Here We Go, was broadcast on the BBC Light Programme the following day. The band were paid a fee of £26 18s plus the cost of four return rail tickets.

It wasn't until October that The Beatles (complete with new drummer Ringo Starr) signed a deal with Brian Epstein and released their debut, Love Me Do.

In 1994 Apple records released a compilation album, Live at the BBC, with 56 songs and 13 tracks of dialogue from interviews originally broadcast on various BBC radio shows.

Fun anagram!
Change cruelty into a word for knives, forks and spoons

Answer: Cutlery

Money-saving tip

The average UK household spends more than £150 a year on cleaning products, but you can get 200-300g of baking soda for a few pounds, which is a great stain cleaner, while white vinegar can be used diluted to clean surfaces, and salt can clean drains and brighten up your laundry.

Mood boosters

Boost your self image – instead of dwelling on your perceived flaws, think about your good qualities. Pick one physical and one personal quality you've been complimented on – be it your eyes, your smile, your kindness or your quick thinking – and practise thinking about these to trick your brain into operating more positively.

A PHOTO TO TREASURE

Here are my wonderful grandparents, Tom and Doris. They are holding their dog, Jodie, and first grandchild, John. I remember how proud Granddad was, striding ahead, pushing John's pram along the lane. They passed on to me a love of gardening and of wildlife. I miss them so much!

Angela Keeler, via email

Recipe of the week

STRAWBERRY ROSE CHEESECAKE

MAKES: **1 cheesecake** PREP: **15 mins** COOK: **N/A**

400g (14oz) digestive biscuits (crushed into crumbs)
200g (7oz) salted butter (melted)
250ml (8fl oz) cream
600g (21oz) cream cheese
400g (14oz) sifted icing sugar
Pinch of vanilla extract
150ml (5fl oz) Tequila Rose
150g (5oz) strawberries (chopped)

1. Mix together the digestive crumbs and melted butter, then layer on the bottom of a cake tin. Leave to chill for 15 mins.
2. In a separate bowl, add the cream then combine with the cream cheese, icing sugar and vanilla extract until the texture is silky and smooth. Add the Tequila Rose and chopped strawberries.
3. Top the crumb base with the creamy strawberry mixture and smooth out. Pop in the fridge overnight.
4. Before serving, pop it in the freezer for an hour before taking it out of the tin to help it solidify. Once out of the tin, let it come to room temperature, serve and enjoy.

@CATANDJAMES WITH TEQUILA ROSE

10 SUNDAY

11 MONDAY

12 TUESDAY

13 WEDNESDAY

14 THURSDAY

15 FRIDAY

16 SATURDAY

On this week...

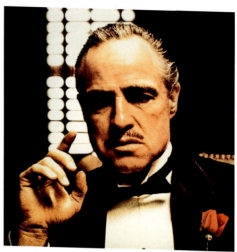

March 14th 1972

AN OFFER YOU CAN'T REFUSE

The first instalment of Francis Ford Coppola's gangster trilogy, The Godfather, premiered in New York. Based on the novel by Mario Puzo, the film tells the story of the powerful Italian-American Corleone family, focusing on the transformation of youngest son Michael (Al Pacino) from reluctant outsider to an utterly ruthless mafia boss.

The film received overwhelming critical acclaim, not least because it features memorable performances from a host of stars including James Caan, Robert Duvall, Sterling Hayden and, perhaps most famously, Marlon Brando as patriarch Don Vito Corleone.

An instant hit, The Godfather became the highest grossing film of 1972 and, after 23 consecutive weeks at No.1, became the fastest film to achieve ticket sales in excess of $101 million. At the following year's Academy Awards The Godfather received a total of 11 nominations before taking home the Oscars for Best Picture, Best Screenplay and Best Actor.

Fun anagram!
Change thing into a time of day

Answer: Night

Money-saving tip

Eco settings on washing machines and dishwashers might not seem very eco when they run for 3½ hours, but using them does save you money. An eco-setting on a dishwasher uses around 20-40 per cent less water than normal programs, which could save you £300 in its lifetime.

Mood boosters

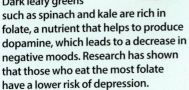

Your parents were right – it's good to eat your green! Dark leafy greens such as spinach and kale are rich in folate, a nutrient that helps to produce dopamine, which leads to a decrease in negative moods. Research has shown that those who eat the most folate have a lower risk of depression.

A PHOTO TO TREASURE

This photo of my granddaughter Skye was taken on her first birthday at her home in Vancouver. She calls me Nonna as I didn't want to be known by any of the usual 'grandma' names. Although I am able to see and hear her on Skype I miss her lovely 'huggles'.

Winifred Abrahams, via email

Recipe of the week

VEGAN CAULIFLOWER & LEEK FILO TARTS

SERVES: **4** PREP: **15 mins** COOK: **20 mins**

1 head cauliflower, cut into florets
1 large leek, green ends included, diced
½ tsp smoked paprika
½ tsp turmeric
½ tsp cumin powder
1 tsp sea salt
1 tbsp olive oil
1 pack of filo pastry sheets, cut into quarters
2 tbsp melted vegan butter
3-4tbsp cranberry sauce, to serve
For the cheese sauce:
2 tbsp vegan butter
200ml (7fl oz) oat milk
½ tsp garlic powder
½ tsp Dijon mustard
75g (3oz) vegan cheese

1. Preheat the oven to 200C/180C Fan/Gas Mark 6.
2. Start by chopping the cauliflower into florets, dice the leek and add to a baking tray. Coat in the spices, salt and oil, then pop in the oven for 15 mins.
3. Prepare the cheese sauce by adding the ingredients to a pot and stirring on a low heat until a thick sauce forms.
4. Slice the filo pastry sheets in half, then half again and grease a muffin tray to fit 8 pastry tarts.
5. Once the cauliflower and leeks have roasted, turn the oven up to 220C/200C Fan/Gas Mark 7 and add the veg to the pot holding the cheesy sauce. Stir until coated.
6. Add around four squares of pastry sheets to each muffin tray, coated with a brush of the melted vegan butter. Once four layers are in add the curried cauliflower mix until it's just level with the top.
7. Pop back in the oven for around 20-23 mins, or until the pastry is golden (your oven may differ).
8. Serve with cranberry sauce and enjoy.

BRITISH LEEKS

17 SUNDAY

18 MONDAY

19 TUESDAY

20 WEDNESDAY

21 THURSDAY

22 FRIDAY

23 SATURDAY

On this week...

March 19th 1953

HOLLYWOOD'S FINEST

The 25th Academy Awards was the first to be held simultaneously at the RKO Pantages Theatre in Hollywood and the NBC International Theatre in New York City. It was also the first Oscars to be broadcast live across US TV and radio networks to an estimated audience of 34 million. The event was co-hosted by Bob Hope in Los Angeles and Conrad Nagel in New York. UK TV networks, which at the time operated on a different system, had to settle for broadcasting a recording of the ceremony two days later.

The major upset of the night was when Cecil B DeMille's The Greatest Show on Earth beat hotly tipped High Noon to Best Motion Picture. But the popular western didn't miss out; Gary Cooper took the Best Actor gong for his role as Marshal Will Kane. John Ford secured his record-breaking fourth win for Best Director for The Quiet Man and Shirley Booth beat Joan Crawford and Bette Davis to Best Actress. The biggest winner was The Bad and the Beautiful, which took five gongs.

Fun anagram!
Change heart into a planet

Answer: Earth

Money-saving tip

Most vegetables survive well in the freezer, so if you see them on offer and have the money and space, consider buying in bulk so you can freeze them raw or turn them into a soup to be divided into batches and then frozen.

Mood boosters

Have a mindful moment. Breathe in and focus on how it feels – the air moving through your nose, your chest rising – then breathe out. Allow your mind to travel around your body, and focus on the present. If a distracting thought arrives, acknowledge it, then let it pass away.

A PHOTO TO TREASURE

This precious photo of me with my daughter Helen was taken in 1977. She had just had her evening feed and was tucked up in her cot with her little pink dog, ready for sleep. It shows the strong bond of love between mother and daughter which never fades.

Julia Christopher, via email

Recipe of the week

ROAST LEG OF LAMB WITH CALIFORNIA WALNUT AND APRICOT CRUST

SERVES: **6** PREP: **15 mins** COOK: **2 hours plus resting**

Whole leg of lamb (2kg/4-5lb)
4 spring onions, roughly chopped + 2 extra
2 sprigs rosemary, leaves only
100g (4oz) California Walnuts + 25g (1oz)
75g (3oz) dried apricots + 25g (1oz)
1 clove garlic
2 tbsp rapeseed oil + 1 tsp
50g (2oz) fresh breadcrumbs
1 tsp white wine vinegar
1 sprig mint, leaves chopped

1. Preheat the oven to 180C/160 Fan/Gas Mark 4. Remove the lamb from the fridge, pat dry with kitchen paper and place in a large roasting tin. Make 6 x 6cm long deep slits in the meat and set aside.
2. Place 4 spring onions, rosemary, 100g (4oz) walnuts, 75g (3oz) apricots and garlic in a food processor with the 2 tbsp of oil and blitz to a coarse crumb. Mix into the breadcrumbs and season.
3. Press some of the crust mix into the slits of the lamb and press the remaining over the top of the joint. Roast for 1 hour then cover with foil and cook for a further hour to give medium rare. Remove from the oven and rest for 15 mins, still covered in foil, before carving.
4. Meanwhile, mix the remaining sliced spring onions, chopped walnuts and diced apricots with 1 tsp oil, 1 tsp white wine vinegar and mint. Serve with the leg of lamb.

CALIFORNIA WALNUTS

24 SUNDAY

25 MONDAY

26 TUESDAY

27 WEDNESDAY

28 THURSDAY

29 FRIDAY

30 SATURDAY

On this week...

March 25th 1973

HIGH-FLYING COMEDY

Viewers of BBC2 were treated to their first look at Ronnie Barker as miserly shopkeeper Arkwright and David Jason as his hapless nephew, Granville. The pilot episode of Open All Hours, written by Roy Clarke, was shown as part of an anthology series called Seven of One. Developed to showcase both the comic talents of Ronnie Barker and the country's best writers, Seven Of One featured seven separate comedies that would serve as possible pilots for sitcoms.

The first episode turned out to be a winner as Arkwright indulges his two main loves – making money from his customers, and pursuing Nurse Gladys Emmanuel (Lynda Baron). Meanwhile his beleaguered errand boy just wants a girlfriend. It was a comic creation that we took to our hearts, and between 1976 and 1985 we were treated to 26 more episodes.

Open All Hours wasn't the only successful pilot from the series. Episode two saw career criminal Norman Stanley Fletcher on his way to serve a five-year sentence at Slade Prison...

Fun anagram!
Change flog into a sport

Answer: Golf

Money-saving tip

Install a "save a flush" bag, which helps use less water each time you flush the toilet. Some water providers will send you one for free. A water-saving shower head can cut the amount of water you use for a shower by up to 50 per cent.

Mood boosters

Being in a green space has been proven to boost your mood – so much so that ecotherapy has been hailed as a positive treatment for anxiety. If you're struggling to get out, even watching greenery on a screen or in a book can help – looking at pictures of outdoor greenery can improve your concentration levels too.

A PHOTO TO TREASURE

Here I am with my very first friend, Linda. Her family moved away and we lost touch. As a teenager I saw her a few times as her school was close by. I was smitten but too shy to speak. Later we met again by chance and we recently celebrated our 53rd anniversary.

Tony Hoare, via email

Recipe of the week

EASTER CAKE

SERVES: **16** PREP: **30 mins** COOK: **40 mins**

380g (13oz) plain flour
3 tsp baking powder
1 ½ tsp baking soda
¼ tsp salt
1 ½ tsp cinnamon
1 tsp ground ginger
1 tsp mixed spice
150g (5oz) brown sugar
140g (5oz) granulated sugar
90g (3oz) Horlicks Original
200ml (7fl oz) vegetable oil
150g (5oz) apple sauce
6 eggs
400g (14oz) grated carrots
300g (11oz) cream cheese, room temperature
200g (7oz) unsalted butter, softened
2 tsp vanilla extract
2 tbsp Horlicks Original
650g (23oz) icing sugar

1. Preheat the oven to 175C/160C Fan/Gas Mark 4.
2. Line three 20cm cake pans with baking paper.
3. In a large mixing bowl, whisk together the dry ingredients, including the sugar.
4. Add the oil, apple sauce and two eggs into the dry ingredients and mix using an electric mixer until combined.
5. Add another two eggs and mix again to fully incorporate them, then mix in the remaining two eggs until the mixture is smooth.
6. Fold in the grated carrots and divide the mixture evenly between the three prepared pans.
7. Bake each cake for 35-40 mins. Leave to cool.
8. To make the frosting, mix together the cream cheese and butter until fluffy.
9. Add vanilla, Horlicks Original and half of the icing sugar and mix until completely combined.
10. Add the rest of the icing sugar and mix for a few mins until light and fluffy.

@MUFFINMUNCHIES

31 SUNDAY

1 MONDAY

2 TUESDAY

3 WEDNESDAY

4 THURSDAY

5 FRIDAY

6 SATURDAY

On this week...

April 2nd 1962

PANDAS ON THE ROAD

A new style of pedestrian crossing caused chaos following its launch in London. The first panda crossing was officially opened in York Road, opposite Waterloo Station by Transport Minister Ernest Marples. It was one of 45 set up at selected sites across the country as part of an experiment as 'a new idea in pedestrian safety'. The panda crossing, which featured black and white triangular markings and a sequence of flashing lights, was devised to replace the zebra crossing.

The police and road safety groups believed that the pedestrian-operated system of lights would ultimately be safer than the zebra crossing, which relied entirely on drivers noticing someone waiting to cross the road.

Sadly, it caused utter confusion and was later abandoned after being beset by multiple technical and mechanical failures.

The pelican crossing, which used a more sophisticated traffic light system, was later introduced in 1969 and this proved much more successful.

Fun anagram!

Change **disease** into a popular place to go on holiday

Answer: Seaside

Money-saving tip

If you have a supermarket loyalty card, don't simply redeem the points against your weekly shopping bill – you'll get better discounts if you convert them to use as discounts for meals, cinema tickets or museum tickets. Remember to collect the points at other shops too (for instance collect Nectar points at Argos and Ebay).

Mood boosters

Feel uplifted with a quick sniff of your fruit bowl. Citrus scents, such as orange, lemon and grapefruit, encourage positive chemical reactions in your brain. Or use a few drops of essential citrus oil on your pulse points. Mixing essential citrus oil with a floral one such as jasmine will increase positive effects.

A PHOTO TO TREASURE

This is Princess Mary House on the Foxlease estate in Hampshire. I first went there aged 19, the youngest in a group of Brownie Guiders. I was nervous at first but loved the experience and have been back many times as a Guider, a Commissioner and a Trainer.

June Jones, Ringwood

Recipe of the week

ASPARAGUS, SMOKED SALMON AND EGG TART

MAKES: **15 squares** PREP: **10 mins plus 10 mins cooling time** COOK: **20 mins**

1 x 320g (11oz) sheet puff pastry
4 medium British Lion eggs
200g (7oz) asparagus spears
150g (5oz) cream cheese, softened
150g (5oz) smoked salmon
A small bunch chives, finely chopped

1. Preheat the oven to 220C/200C Fan/Gas Mark 7. Unroll the puff pastry sheet and place on its paper onto a baking tray. Using a sharp, small knife cut a 1.5cm border around the edges (making sure not to cut all the way through). Prick the inside of the pastry all over with a fork.
2. Place in the oven and bake for 20 mins, until golden and puffed. Remove from the oven and, using a spoon, carefully push the inside of the pastry back down. Leave to cool for 10 mins.
3. Meanwhile, bring a medium pan of water to the boil and add the eggs. Boil for 7 mins then drain under cold water to cool. Peel and cut into quarters.
4. Add the asparagus to the boiling water along with a generous pinch of salt and cook for 5-7 mins until soft, but still with a little bite. Drain under cold water to cool and set aside.
5. Spread the inside of the pastry with the cream cheese. Top with the asparagus spears, smoked salmon and quartered eggs. Season lightly and sprinkle over the chives. Cut into 15 squares to serve.

BRITISH LION EGGS

7 SUNDAY

8 MONDAY

9 TUESDAY

10 WEDNESDAY

11 THURSDAY

12 FRIDAY

13 SATURDAY

On this week...

April 7th 1973

EUROVISION RETURN

Cliff Richard represented the UK in the 18th Eurovision Song Contest. He performed Power to All Our Friends, a song which had been chosen by BBC viewers after Cliff performed six contending songs on Cilla Black's Saturday evening TV show. Written by Guy Fletcher and Doug Flett, the song was awarded a total of 123 points by the international jury, securing third place for the UK in a closely fought competition. The winner was Anne-Marie David with 129 points for host country Luxembourg.

Security for the contest was tight as there were fears of a terrorist attack in light of the events at the Munich Olympics the previous year. Terry Wogan, the UK's long-serving commentator, recalled the floor manager strongly advising the audience to stay seated for risk of being shot by security forces.

The 1973 contest was the most-watched in the UK with an estimated 21.54 million tuning in. This was Cliff's second Eurovision entry, having previously taken second place in 1968.

Fun anagram!

Change **recall** into one of the rooms in a house

Answer: Cellar

Money-saving tip

Challenge yourself to have 'No Spend Days'. This not only stops you impulse shopping but helps you to think creatively – if you regularly meet a friend for coffee, take a flask and suggest a walk instead. Google 'free things to do' in your area and see how long you can go without spending!

Mood boosters

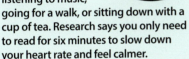

Reading calms your mind more effectively than activities such as listening to music, going for a walk, or sitting down with a cup of tea. Research says you only need to read for six minutes to slow down your heart rate and feel calmer.

A PHOTO TO TREASURE

This is the entire cast of a play produced by my school, St Wilfrid's Convent in Exeter. All the pupils from the infants to the seniors were involved. There were a lot of rehearsals but also a lot of fun before it was performed before an audience of friends and relatives.

Sheila Mills, Minehead

Recipe of the week

SPICY LAMB FLATBREADS

SERVES: **12** PREP: **5 mins** COOK: **7 mins**

6 oval flatbreads/large pita breads
425g (15oz) crème fraiche
340g (12oz) aubergine cardamom jam or tomato sauce or your favourite sundried tomato paste
800g (28oz) roasted lamb shoulder, torn
Olive oil
170g (6oz) chermoula paste
170g (6oz) tahini
3-4 tsp Banhoek chili oil to taste
1 bunch Italian parsley, roughly chopped
32g (1oz) toasted pine nuts

1. Preheat the oven to 200C/180C Fan/Gas Mark 6. Lay the flatbreads on lined baking trays.
2. Spread the flatbreads with a good dessertspoonful of crème fraiche. Spread or dollop the tomato sauce over the crème fraiche. Layer the torn lamb on top of these two layers.
3. Drizzle the olive oil over the torn lamb. Pop the flatbreads in the hot oven for 5-7 mins.
4. When you remove the flatbreads from the oven, drizzle with the chermoula.
5. Zig zag a good spoonful of tahini over the flatbread. Sprinkle with the chili oil to taste and top with the roughly chopped parsley and toasted pine nuts.
6. Cut into easy-to-eat pieces and arrange on a board.

BANHOEK CHILI OIL

14 SUNDAY

15 MONDAY

16 TUESDAY

17 WEDNESDAY

18 THURSDAY

19 FRIDAY

20 SATURDAY

On this week...

April 16th 1972

A WELCOME GIFT

Pandas Ling-Ling and Hsing-Hsing were sent to the United States as a gesture of friendship from the Chinese government following a visit by President Nixon. First Lady Pat Nixon donated the pair to the National Zoo in Washington DC. More than 20,000 people visited the pandas on their first day and an estimated 1.1 million people saw them during their first year in the United States.

The pandas were wildly popular and China's gift was a huge diplomatic success. The People's Republic of China began to regularly use 'panda diplomacy', and between 1957 and 1983 gifted 24 pandas to nine nations as gestures of friendship.

During their time at the zoo, the pair had five cubs, but sadly none of them survived past a few days. Ling-Ling lived until 1992, at which time she was the longest-lived giant panda in captivity outside China. Hsing-Hsing lived until 1999. The Panda House was then empty until the arrival of Mei Xiang and Tian Tian in December 2000.

Fun anagram!
Change cheap into a fruit

Answer: Peach

Money-saving tip

If your car boot is full of things you've been meaning to take to the tip, or it's just being used as extra storage, clear it out. Also take off an empty roof rack as both of these can increase fuel costs by 12 per cent.

Mood boosters

Get your hands dirty this spring – breathing in the smell of soil has been found to give your spirits a lift. The bacteria in soil produces similar effects to antidepressant drugs by stimulating the release of the feel-good hormone serotonin. Your garden will appreciate your handywork too!

A PHOTO TO TREASURE

This photo of my mum and dad, Maureen and John Chilton, was taken in 1964 when they were guests at a friend's wedding. I think they make a very handsome couple! Having met at a dance evening, they will be celebrating their diamond wedding anniversary this year.

Esther Chilton, via email

Recipe of the week

BRAISED PEAS WITH CALIFORNIA WALNUTS & PANCETTA

SERVES: **4-6** PREP: **10 mins** COOK: **10 mins**

½ tbsp rapeseed oil
150g (5oz) smoked diced pancetta
5 spring onions, sliced
300g (11oz) frozen peas
1 clove garlic, crushed
50g (2oz) California Walnuts, roughly chopped
300ml (10 fl oz) chicken stock
2 sprigs mint, leaves only
1 tsp Dijon mustard

1. Heat the oil in a large frying pan and fry the pancetta for 3 mins until crispy. Drain off most of the excess oil. Add the spring onions, peas and garlic and fry for a further 3 mins.
2. Stir in the walnuts, stock, mint and Dijon and cook for 2-3 mins.

CALIFORNIA WALNUTS

21 SUNDAY

22 MONDAY

23 TUESDAY

24 WEDNESDAY

25 THURSDAY

26 FRIDAY

27 SATURDAY

On this week...

April 26th 1982

BATTLE FOR THE FALKLANDS

Just a matter of weeks after hostilities began, Britain re-established a presence in the Falkland Islands. Following a two-hour assault, Royal Marines were able to re-take the remote island of South Georgia. In a statement, Defence Secretary Mr Nott said Argentine forces surrendered to the British troops with "only limited resistance".

There were no British casualties reported in the operation. Argentina's military junta had invaded the remote South Atlantic colony on April 2, claiming it had sovereignty, having inherited the islands from Spain in the 1800s.

The UK, which had ruled the islands for 150 years, quickly chose to rush to the defence of the islanders. Prime Minister Margaret Thatcher reacted strongly, sending a task force of 28,000 troops and over 100 ships to reclaim the islands. By contrast, Argentina had 12,000 mainly conscripted soldiers and just 40 ships. The Argentines surrendered on June 14, as British troops marched into Stanley and the town was liberated.

Fun anagram!

Change hated into something that comes to everybody

Answer: Death

Money-saving tip

Before buying electrical items, check out Amazon Warehouse, where all its returns are sold with big discounts. You'll get an idea of an item's condition before buying it, but often it's just the odd blemish on the box or some cosmetic wear-and-tear. You still have a right to return the goods in 30 days, just as you normally would at Amazon.

Mood boosters

Start your day with an instant win by making your bed! Studies have shown that by succeeding in the first task of your day, you're more likely to set yourself up to complete tasks later in the day, and will benefit from a feeling of achievement and control! Now fluff those pillows!

A PHOTO TO TREASURE

Here is a photo of me taken in 1976 when I was 20. I used to think I looked very trendy as I left the house and ignored my brother when he joked: "Who blacked your eyes?" My father used to say: "Bye love, oh, your collar's turned up!"

Bren Morris, via email

Recipe of the week

GINGER CAKE WITH LEMON GLAZE ICING

SERVES: **9** PREP: **15 mins** COOK: **45 mins**

For the cake:
200g (7oz) butter, softened
125g (4oz) The Groovy Food Company Agave Nectar Rich and Dark
200g (7oz) golden syrup
200g (7oz) black treacle
400g (14oz) self-raising flour, sifted
3 tsp ground ginger
4 pieces of stem ginger, chopped finely
2 free-range eggs, beaten
For the icing:
150g (5oz) icing sugar
Juice of 2 lemons
Zest of 1 lemon

1. Line and grease a 23cm/9in square tin. Preheat the oven to 160C/140C Fan/Gas Mark 3.
2. Place the butter, The Groovy Food Company Agave Rich and Dark, syrup and treacle in a pan and heat gently until melted. Set aside.
3. Sift the flour and ginger into a bowl, add the stem ginger and mix.

Pour the cooled butter mixture into the flour. Add the eggs and beat until well combined.

4. Pour the cake batter into the tin and level the surface. Bake for 45-50 mins, or until the cake has risen and is golden brown. Set aside to cool slightly in the tin, then transfer to a wire rack and set aside to cool.
5. To make the lemon icing, sift the icing sugar into a bowl. Add about two tablespoons of the juice from a lemon and mix to a smooth paste. Add more lemon until you get a smooth but runny icing. Pour the icing over the cooled cake and spread lightly, allowing it to ooze over the edges. Sprinkle over chopped lemon zest and set the cake aside until the icing has set. Cut into 9 pieces (3x3 in squares).

THE GROOVY FOOD COMPANY

28 SUNDAY

29 MONDAY

30 TUESDAY

1 WEDNESDAY

2 THURSDAY

3 FRIDAY

4 SATURDAY

On this week...

April 30th 1972

FAREWELL TO THE BELLE

The Brighton Belle, a flagship of the Southern Railways fleet, made her final journey from London's Victoria station to Brighton on the Sussex coast.

The service, which had run largely uninterrupted since January 1933, was refurbished and overhauled in 1955 but, despite protests, it was thought that by 1972 the carriages offered a poor ride by contemporary standards.

A campaign to return the Brighton Belle to mainline service was launched in 2009. After undergoing a ten-year revamp and costing six million pounds, the 1930s train has now almost been restored to its former glory. Much effort has been made to preserve its authentic art deco design, however there have been some unavoidable changes made to make the historic train compatible with modern transport.

It is unknown when the Belle will be fully operational and back on the rails, but we hope we won't have to wait too much longer!

Fun anagram!
Change super into something you keep money in

Answer: Purse

Mood boosters

According to colour psychology, your choice of hues in your home can affect your mood. If you want to feel energised, pick warm orange, yellow or green tones. There's no need to redecorate your house – just the addition of a simple vase or cushion can lift an area.

A PHOTO TO TREASURE

This is a photo of my wonderful mum and dad, Violet and Leonard, on their wedding day in 1951. I think they look like film stars. Both of them were born in Hackney where they met at a dance club called Fred's. They were happily married for 54 years.

Christine Veal, via email

Recipe of the week

GNOCCHI WITH ROAST VEGETABLES

SERVES: **4** PREP: **20 mins** COOK: **30 mins**

500g (18oz) potato gnocchi
400g (14oz) Brussels sprouts (frozen or fresh)
1 zucchini cut into cubes or half rounds or florets of a small broccoli
250g (9oz) cherry tomatoes
1 red onion
1 tbsp Italian seasoning or dried herbs of choice
3 whole garlic cloves, whole or crushed
Olive oil and lemon juice to drizzle
Salt and freshly ground pepper for seasoning
4 streaks of pancetta or smoked bacon cut into thin slices

1. Preheat your oven to 200C/180C Fan/Gas Mark 6.
2. Place the gnocchi and the defrosted and drained vegetables, onion, herbs and garlic in a bowl and drizzle with olive oil and lemon juice. Season with salt and pepper.
3. Stir everything carefully to coat with the oil and lemon juice.
4. Transfer onto a baking paper-lined oven tray and space apart using a spatula.
5. Sprinkle over the bacon bits (this is optional).
6. Bake for 30-35 mins, turning everything over with a spatula half way through baking time and remove when vegetables are crisp and slightly browned. Serve warm on its own or with crusty bread.

UK HEALTHY LIVING AND AGEING PLATFORM GOLDSTER

5 SUNDAY

6 MONDAY

7 TUESDAY

8 WEDNESDAY

9 THURSDAY

10 FRIDAY

11 SATURDAY

On this week...

May 5th 1962

RECORD-BREAKER

The soundtrack album for the film West Side Story went to No.1 in the US album charts, where it stayed for a record-breaking 54 weeks. The album soon hit the No.1 spot in the UK charts too, selling more than 100,000 copies. It remains one of the most popular soundtrack recordings of all time featuring such iconic tracks as Maria and I Feel Pretty – all written by Leonard Bernstein, with lyrics by Stephen Sondheim.

The film had launched the year before and we'd fallen head over heels for the tragic story of Tony and Maria, the star-crossed lovers who were brought together by chance but kept apart by prejudice.

This was our chance to enjoy their story again in the comfort of our own homes, but reading the sleeve notes for the album revealed a few surprises, as some of the stars of the film had had their singing over-dubbed. Natalie Wood, who played Maria, had her parts sung by Marni Nixon, while Jimmy Bryant dubbed the role of Tony for Richard Beymer.

Fun anagram!
Change flow into an animal

Answer: Wolf

Money-saving tip

Your microwave is an efficient cooking method, but if it's left plugged in, with the display lit up at all hours of the day and night, it's consuming power. Switching it off at the wall when not in use can save around £6 a year in electricity.

Mood boosters

The phrase "fake it 'til you make it" sounds cheesy, but research has shown that it's true. The simple act of smiling – even when you don't feel like it – can help to activate the happiness centre in your brain. It's worth trying this simple pick-me-up.

A PHOTO TO TREASURE

This photo shows my dear late wife, Iris, and me on our wedding day in 1956. Iris' wedding dress of figured brocade was tailor-made by a seamstress. My grey suit was from the Fifty Shilling Tailors. The limo we'd hired couldn't wait so we had to leave in the photographer's van!

Derrick Woodward, via email

Recipe of the week

CALIFORNIA WALNUT CRUSTED VEGAN BREAD

MAKES: **1 loaf** PREP: **20 mins** COOK: **45 mins**

250ml (8fl oz) dairy alternative milk, such as oat milk
1 tbsp cider vinegar
250g (9oz) whole California Walnuts
150g (5oz) wholemeal flour
150g (5oz) plain flour
1 tsp baking powder
1 tsp bicarbonate of soda

1. Preheat the oven to 180C/160C/Gas Mark 4 and grease an 8½ x 4½in loaf pan. Set it aside.
2. Whisk together the milk and cider vinegar in a jug, and set it aside for 5 mins to turn into buttermilk.
3. Place 200g (7oz) of the California Walnuts in a blender and blend until the walnuts are ground.
   Then transfer to a large mixing bowl. Sieve the two flours, baking powder and bicarbonate of soda in the bowl, and mix together well. Make a well in the centre of the bowl.
4. Pour the buttermilk into the well of the dry ingredients, using your free hand to mix the flour into the buttermilk. Make sure there are no dry patches and that the dough is completely wet.
5. Pour the bread mixture into the prepared loaf tin.
6. Roughly chop the remaining whole walnuts and sprinkle on top of the bread, using your hand to gently push them into the mixture.
7. Bake in the pre-heated oven for 45 mins or until a toothpick inserted into the centre comes out clean. If the top is starting to brown, but the inside is still soft, you can cover the top with tinfoil.

CLODAGH MCKENNA FOR CALIFORNIA WALNUTS

12 SUNDAY

13 MONDAY

14 TUESDAY

15 WEDNESDAY

16 THURSDAY

17 FRIDAY

18 SATURDAY

On this week...

May 18th 1972

A FINAL VISIT

The Queen and Prince Philip travelled, along with Prince Charles, to Paris to meet with Edward, Duke of Windsor and his wife, Wallis Simpson, now a duchess. He was unfortunately in poor health and unable to greet them formally, but he was able to spend a few precious minutes with his niece.

The royal party were on a state visit to France and took the opportunity to see Edward for the first time in five years.

Although tensions had thawed somewhat, they remained between the duke, his wife and certain members of the royal family. Queen Mary, for example, refused to ever receive the duchess formally, which meant Edward never achieved his dearest wish – to have the title of Royal Highness conferred on her.

The duke had undergone a hernia operation earlier in the year and his health later took a turn for the worse. Ten days after Elizabeth II's visit the duke died. Doctors later revealed that he had been suffering from throat cancer for some time.

Fun anagram!
Change **keen** into a part of the body

Answer: Knee

Money-saving tip

Before paying full price for an item, consider haggling! Most hagglers have around 39 per cent success rate, saving £155 per person on average per year, so it's worth a punt. If something has a mark on it or an electrical item has a damaged box, ask if you can get a discount.

Mood boosters

Try a mindful walk – simply walk and connect to the here and now. Ask yourself: what can I see? What can I hear? What can I feel? Really tune into what's around you, using all your senses. Just being outdoors will release endorphins, those feel-good hormones that are good for your mental health.

A PHOTO TO TREASURE

This is my mum, Beryl (on the left) with her mum, Elsie. They both look so elegant. We think Mum was in her 20s when this photo was taken. She is in her 90s now and wishes she had hair like that! She is still just as beautiful, though.

Hilary Biggs, via email

Recipe of the week

HOUMOUS, COURGETTE AND AUBERGINE TART

SERVES: **6 - 8** PREP: **5 mins** COOK: **30 mins**

400g (14oz) tin of chickpeas
1 tbsp tahini
Extra virgin olive oil
1 tbsp Tracklements Green Tomato Chutney
2 courgettes, cut into rounds 5mm thick
1 aubergine, cut into rounds 5mm thick
Salt and pepper
320g (11oz) ready-made shortcrust pastry
Parmesan, grated

1. Preheat the oven to 180C/160 Fan/Gas Mark 4 and put a baking tray on the middle shelf.
2. Drain the chickpeas and whizz in a food processor with the tahini, oil and Green Tomato Chutney until it becomes a smooth paste.
3. Heat a tbsp of oil in a frying pan over a medium-high heat. Add the courgettes and aubergine in a single layer and season. Make sure they don't overlap. Cook for 3-4 mins, turn and cook for a further 3-4 mins. Remove from the heat and transfer to a piece of kitchen towel on a warm plate. Continue in batches until cooked and golden.
4. Grease a 20cm fluted tart tin. Roll out the pastry on a floured surface to the thickness of a £1 coin and about 2cm bigger than the tin. Line the tin with the pastry. Chill for 15 mins.
5. Take the tart out of the fridge, line with baking parchment (scrunch it up first to make it more pliable), then fill with baking beans. Bake for 10 mins, then remove the beans and parchment and bake for 5 mins more until the pastry is golden. Allow to cool and carefully trim off any excess pastry.
6. Spread the houmous evenly over the cooled crust and arrange alternate rounds of courgette and aubergine slices over the top. Sprinkle with parmesan and bake in the oven for 5 mins until hot.

TRACKLEMENTS

19 SUNDAY

20 MONDAY

21 TUESDAY

22 WEDNESDAY

23 THURSDAY

24 FRIDAY

25 SATURDAY

On this week...

May 23, 1983

MAY THE FORCE BE WITH YOU

The premiere of the final instalment of the original Star Wars trilogy took place in New York. Return of the Jedi sees Han Solo (Harrison Ford), Luke Skywalker (Mark Hamill) and Princess Leia (Carrie Fisher) battling with the dark forces of the Galactic Empire.

The film took $374 million at the box office and became the year's highest grossing film. The film was well-received by critics, with strong praise going to the special effects and action sequences, performances, John Williams' score, and emotional weight.

Several re-releases and revisions to the film have followed over the decades, which has also brought its total gross to $482 million.

Fun anagram!
Change **break** into a job

Answer: Baker

Money-saving tip

Always look to see if there are codes available on voucher sites to get money off with retailers before buying something. Sometimes, if you sign up for an account with a retailer online, you'll be offered a discount when you sign up to its newsletter.

Mood boosters

Sing for happiness! University of Manchester researchers discovered that a tiny organ in the inner ear (called the sacculus) is connected to a part of the brain that registers pleasure. The sacculus detects frequency notes associated with singing and, almost instantly, gives you a lovely warm and fuzzy feeling.

A PHOTO TO TREASURE

My lovely cherry red coat was purchased from Long Tall Sally in Manchester in 1988. It was in the sale for £65, less than half the original price. I still get compliments when I wear it every winter. The scarf I'm wearing is also over 30 years old.

Madeleine Freelove, via email

Recipe of the week

PEACH, HONEY AND ROSEMARY COBBLER

SERVES: **4-6** PREP: **25 mins** COOK: **30 mins**

A little soft butter
2 cans (415g) Del Monte® Peach Slices in Juice
1 tsp finely chopped rosemary (or use grated orange or lemon zest)
2 tbsp runny honey
Ingredients for the cobbler topping:
100g (4oz) self-raising wholemeal flour
Pinch of salt
35g (1oz) cold butter, diced
35g (1oz) caster sugar
50g (2oz) ground almonds
1 medium egg
4 tbsp milk

1. Preheat the oven to 190C/170C Fan/Gas Mark 5. Butter a 1.5 litre capacity oven dish.
2. Drain the peach slices, reserving 2 tbsp of the juice. Arrange in the dish, scatter with rosemary, then trickle over the reserved juice and the honey.
3. To make the topping, put the flour and salt into a mixing bowl or a food processor, add the butter and rub it in with your fingers, or process until the mix resembles crumbs. Stir or blitz in the sugar and ground almonds. Beat the egg and the milk together then stir into the flour mix to make a soft, sticky dough.
4. Drop the dough over the fruit in small spoonfuls – the topping shouldn't cover all the fruit.
5. Bake for 30 mins until the 'cobbles' are cooked through (test one with a skewer and check it comes out clean). Serve hot, warm or cold with double cream.

DEL MONTE®

26 SUNDAY

27 MONDAY

28 TUESDAY

29 WEDNESDAY

30 THURSDAY

31 FRIDAY

1 SATURDAY

On this week...

May 29th 1973

ANNE GETS ENGAGED

Princess Anne announced her engagement to Mark Phillips, who was a lieutenant in 1st The Queen's Dragoon Guards. The couple met at a party in 1968 and shared a love of horses. They both competed for Team GB at the Olympic Games in equestrian events.

Phillips presented Anne with a sapphire and diamond ring after asking her father, The Duke of Edinburgh, for permission to marry.

The couple married in November 1973 at Westminster Abbey. The spectacular wedding was watched by an estimated global audience of 500 million people. Anne wore a high-necked gown by Maureen Baker of London-based label Susan Small and paired it with Queen Mary's Fringe Tiara, which was also worn by Queen Elizabeth on her wedding day in 1947. Mark was offered a royal title by the Queen but he chose to deny the honour, preferring to keep his 'Captain' title. The couple were married for 19 years before eventually divorcing in 1992 and subsequently marrying other people.

Fun anagram!
Change tea into a verb

Answer: Eat

Money-saving tip

Cut the cost of a holiday this summer by ditching the hotel and swapping your home for someone else's. Try house swapping websites such as lovehomeswap.com, trustedhousesitters.com or nomador.com, and you'll have access to thousands of homes in a variety of countries.

Mood boosters

Add some literal spring to your step by walking like Tigger! Next time you're out, adjust your walk to make it more bouncy – it will have a positive impact on your mood (plus it can help burn more calories!).

A PHOTO TO TREASURE

This is me, aged eight, as Her Majesty Queen Elizabeth II. It was June 1953 and I'd been chosen to take part in a pageant to celebrate the Coronation. Our neighbour lent me some clip-on earrings and my dad painted my brown Clarks sandals gold. I was so excited!

Ann Russell, St Neots

Recipe of the week

SPICED EGG, ROASTED CAULIFLOWER AND CHICKPEA SALAD

SERVES: **6** PREP: **10 mins** COOK: **25 mins**

500g (18oz) cauliflower florets
1 large red onion, in chunks
1 large red pepper, in chunks
1 (400g/14oz) can chickpeas
2 tbsp olive oil
2 tsp cumin seeds
1 tsp smoked paprika
½ tsp turmeric
½ tsp chili flakes
Salt and black pepper
6 medium Lion Quality eggs
1 (100g/4oz) bag baby spinach
For the dressing:
4 tbsp Greek yogurt
1 tbsp tahini
1 tbsp olive oil
1 tbsp lemon juice

1. Preheat the oven to 220C/200C Fan/Gas Mark 7. Take a large roasting tin, add the cauliflower, onion, pepper, chickpeas and oil and toss to mix.
2. In a small bowl, mix together all the spices with a little salt and pepper (reserve ½ tsp for garnish), sprinkle the rest over the vegetables in the tray.
3. Toss until evenly coated in the spices. Bake for 25 mins.
4. Put the eggs in a pan and cover with cold water. Bring to the boil, then simmer for 6 mins.
5. Drain the eggs and run them under cold water, tapping the shells as they cool. Once cold enough to handle peel and discard the shells. Cut the eggs in half and leave to cool.
6. Place all the dressing ingredients together in a bowl and mix together with a fork.
7. Remove the vegetables from the oven, add the spinach leaves and half the dressing and mix well or the spinach leaves will wilt. Heap the warm salad onto a large serving dish. Top with the eggs, drizzle over the remaining dressing and the reserved spices.
BRITISH LION EGGS

2 SUNDAY

3 MONDAY

4 TUESDAY

5 WEDNESDAY

6 THURSDAY

7 FRIDAY

8 SATURDAY

On this week...

June 5th 1952

BOWLED OVER!

Freddie Trueman made his Test debut for England in a match against India. Now widely acknowledged as one of the greatest bowlers in cricket history, Trueman was just 21 when he stepped onto the pitch at Headingley to open the bowling with Alec Bedser. England went on to win the match by seven wickets. Trueman deployed a genuinely fast pace and was widely known as 'Fiery Fred'. He was the first bowler to take 300 wickets in a Test career.

His talent, skill and public profile were such that British Prime Minister Harold Wilson jokingly described him as the "greatest living Yorkshireman". Even so, Trueman was omitted from numerous England teams because he was frequently in conflict with the cricket establishment, which he often criticised for its perceived 'snobbishness' and hypocrisy.

After he retired from playing, he became a media personality through his work in television and as an outspoken radio commentator for the BBC.

Fun anagram!
Change swap into an insect

Answer: Wasp

Money-saving tip

When you're driving in warmer weather and need cooling down, don't automatically hit the air conditioning button. If you're travelling at a speed of up to 60 miles and hour, it's best to open a window – above that, it's more effective to use air con.

Mood boosters

Keeping in touch with people is an important factor for wellness but, when you're busy, it's easy to neglect seeing your friends and family. Many studies have linked loneliness to medical issues, such as increasing your risk of high blood pressure and depression. So pick up the phone for a happiness boost.

A PHOTO TO TREASURE

This photo of my three-year-old daughter Olivia and me was taken in Morecambe at the time of the Queen's Platinum Jubilee celebrations. Olivia was so excited by it all that even now when she sees a Union Jack she refers to it as the Jubilee flag!

Justine Machin, via email

Recipe of the week

CRAB LINGUINE

SERVES: **2** PREP: **5 mins** COOK: **20 mins**

250g (9oz) Seggiano Linguine
1 tbsp Lunaio Chilli Oil
1 clove garlic, finely chopped
150g (5oz) cherry tomatoes, halved
100g (4oz) brown crab meat
100g (4oz) white crab meat
½ tsp Seggiano Semi Fresh Parsley
Juice of ½ lemon
Salt and pepper

1. Bring a large pan of water to the boil and add a generous pinch of salt. Add the linguine and cook according to the pack instructions until al dente.
2. Meanwhile, heat the chilli oil in a large pan over a low heat and add the garlic, cook for 2-3 mins, stirring frequently, until softened but not coloured.
3. Add the cherry tomatoes and cook for 4-5 mins until softened then crush with the back of a wooden spoon to release the juices.
4. Add the brown crab meat to the pan, along with a splash of the pasta cooking water and stir to create a silky sauce.
5. Once the pasta is cooked, use a pair of tongs to lift the pasta from the cooking water and into the pan with the crab sauce. Stir to coat the pasta, adding a little more pasta water if needed.
6. Remove from the heat and stir in the white crab meat, semi fresh parsley and lemon juice. Season with salt and pepper to taste.
7. Divide between 2 bowls and serve immediately drizzled with a little extra chilli oil, if liked.

SEGGIANO

9 SUNDAY

10 MONDAY

11 TUESDAY

12 WEDNESDAY

13 THURSDAY

14 FRIDAY

15 SATURDAY

On this week...

June 11th 1962

PRISON BREAK

Three men made a daring escape from California's notorious high-security prison, Alcatraz. Frank Lee Morris and brothers Clarence and John Algin made dummies of themselves out of soap, toilet paper and real hair to place in their beds to fool the guards making night-time inspections. They then cut through the back of their cells using sharpened spoons and crawled on to the roof through ventilation shafts.

It's thought they then made a makeshift raft and floated away from the island. A huge manhunt was launched, including more than 100 armed troops, and police warned members of the public not to approach the men. The convicted bank robbers were never recaptured but opinion is divided as to whether they succeeded in their escape or drowned in San Francisco Bay.

In 1979 their story was dramatised as a film, Escape From Alcatraz, starring Clint Eastwood as Frank Morris, and Patrick McGoohan as the warden.

Fun anagram!

Change bleat into an item of furniture

Answer: Table

Money-saving tip

Check what interest your credit card provider charges before you go on holiday – most charge around three per cent. Avoid these charges by applying for a card with zero transaction fees. Always select the local currency when given the option for payment – you'll save money that way.

Mood boosters

You may not associate how much water you drink with your mood, but dehydration can make you feel short tempered and irritable. Keep a flask or a bottle of water beside you and keep sipping throughout the day. Aim to have 2.5 litres a day, or more if it's very hot.

A PHOTO TO TREASURE

This photo of me and my mum, Alice Madeley, was taken at my Uncle Alec's memorial service. His widow, Auntie Elsie, asked everyone to wear his favourite colour combination of navy and white and we duly obliged. Uncle Alec died in 1973, having survived being gassed in the First World War.

Margaret O'Callaghan, via email

Recipe of the week

MINI LEMON CURD AND BLUEBERRY TARTS

MAKES: **30 mini tarts** PREP: **10 mins, plus 15 mins cooling time** COOK: **15 mins**

3 large British Lion eggs
140g (5oz) caster sugar
3 unwaxed lemons, juiced (150ml/5fl oz) and zested
75g (3oz) unsalted butter, diced
30 blueberries
30 mini tart cases
15g (1oz) unsalted pistachios, very finely chopped, to garnish (optional)

1. Crack two of the eggs and one egg yolk into a medium, heatproof bowl. Place the remaining egg white into a small bowl.
2. Add 100g (4oz) sugar, the lemon juice and zest to the medium bowl and whisk well. Add the butter to the bowl and place the bowl over a pan of simmering water, making sure it doesn't touch the water. Stir the mixture until the butter has melted, around 5 mins. Continue to cook the mixture, stirring continuously with a whisk until it thickens, around 10-15 mins.
3. Remove the bowl from the heat and leave to cool.
4. Meanwhile lightly whisk the egg white with a fork. Sprinkle the remaining sugar on a large plate. Dip a few blueberries at a time into the egg white then toss them in the sugar and set aside. Repeat with the remaining blueberries.
5. Pipe or spoon the curd into the tart cases then top each one with a frosted blueberry. Garnish with pistachios if desired.

BRITISH LION EGGS

16 SUNDAY

17 MONDAY

18 TUESDAY

19 WEDNESDAY

20 THURSDAY

21 FRIDAY

22 SATURDAY

On this week...

June 17th 1972

A PRESIDENTIAL SCANDAL

Five White House operatives were arrested for a break-in at the offices of the Democratic National Committee. Posing as plumbers, the men had entered the Watergate building in order to plant surveillance bugs. It later became clear they'd been funded by President Nixon's re-election campaign committee. Washington Post reporters Bob Woodward and Carl Bernstein uncovered evidence that knowledge of the break-in and attempts to cover it up reached to the highest levels of justice department, the FBI, CIA and the White House. Chief among their sources was an anonymous individual, known only as 'Deep Throat' – later revealed to be William Mark Felt, deputy director of the FBI. Several witnesses later testified that Nixon had approved plans to cover up his administration's involvement in the plot, and there was taped evidence of his involvement.

The ensuing scandal, known as The Watergate Scandal, led to the impeachment and resignation of the President.

Fun anagram!
Change **repaint** into a job

Answer: Painter

Money-saving tip

Warm summers can lead to a lot of plant watering, and high water useage. Cut your bill by using a waterbutt for rainwater plus water-saving gel on your plants – it reduces their watering needs by up to four times by storing water they can extract when they need it.

Mood boosters

When was the last time YOU bought yourself flowers? Studies have found that having fresh flowers in your home helps abate negative moods, plus people who buy themselves flowers felt more compassion towards others. What an easy way to help yourself and others!

A PHOTO TO TREASURE

This photo of my three-year-old granddaughter, Amelia Rose, was taken when she was a flower girl at her cousin Amber's wedding in September 2021. She was patiently waiting for the bride to arrive. I think she looks like a little angel.

Josie Rawson,
Nottingham

Recipe of the week

CHICKEN AND KALE CHILLI

SERVES: **4** PREP: **15 mins** COOK: **30 mins**

1 tbsp oil
1 leek, sliced
1 clove garlic, chopped
2 tsp chilli powder
1 tsp ground cumin
500g (18oz) minced chicken or turkey
2 tbsp tomato puree
400g (14oz) can chopped tomatoes
400g (14oz) can black beans, drained and rinsed
250g (9oz) bag kale
1 ripe avocado, diced
Soured cream and cooked rice to serve

1. Heat the oil in a large saucepan and fry the leek and garlic for 1 min. Add the spices and then the minced chicken (or turkey) and fry until browned.
2. Add the tomato puree and chopped tomatoes along with ½ can of water and the beans. Cover and simmer for 20 mins.
3. Meanwhile, cook the kale in boiling water for 3-4 mins, drain well then stir into the chilli. Season to taste.
4. Serve topped with avocado and a spoonful of soured cream on a bed of rice.

DISCOVER GREAT VEG

23 SUNDAY

24 MONDAY

25 TUESDAY

26 WEDNESDAY

27 THURSDAY

28 FRIDAY

29 SATURDAY

On this week...

June 23rd 2016

THE BIRTH OF BREXIT

It's hard to believe it now but there was a time when the word 'Brexit' didn't exist. The highly recognisable term was coined by the historic referendum that saw Britain vote to leave the EU. In the end, 51.89% of Brits voted in favour of leaving the EU, and 48.11% voted in favour of remaining a member of the EU.

The decision caused a huge shock to the political establishment and led to the resignation of the Prime Minister David Cameron. The value of the pound was highly unstable as it fell to levels not seen since 1985.

The decision spilt the country into those who voted to leave (leavers) and those who wanted to stay (remainers or remoaners as they were often called). It took until December 2020 for a trade deal between the UK and the EU to finally be agreed, nearly four years later.

Fun anagram!
Change **hornet** into a place where Kings and Queens sit

Answer: Throne

Money-saving tip

While on holiday, use a pre-paid currency card to ensure you don't go beyond your holiday budget. That way your currency deal will be locked in from the start so you know where you are and how much you've got to spend.

Mood boosters

Each morning, spend five to ten minutes thinking about everything you feel grateful for. This can be anything, from the fact you have a cosy bed, to your health or something you achieved the previous day. It will elevate your mood, help you relish good experiences and feel more positive.

A PHOTO TO TREASURE

This happy photo of my husband and me was taken at our wedding, over 54 years ago. We were laughing because the knife wouldn't cut through the icing on the cake. We have been laughing together through thick and thin ever since.

Catherine Procter, via email

Recipe of the week

PICNIC PASTIES

SERVES: **12** PREP: **1 hour** COOK: **15 mins**

125g (4oz) Carr's Wholemeal Flour
125g (4oz) Carr's Strong White Flour
6 tbsp vegetable oil
2 red onions
2 tbsp butter
1 tsp brown sugar
1 clove of garlic (crushed)
Balsamic vinegar
2 eating apples (skin on and diced)
125g (4oz) crumbly Lancashire cheese
1 egg (beaten, to glaze)

1. Sift the two flours together and add a pinch of salt. Add 5 tbsp of cold water to the oil and mix with the flour to form a dough. Knead lightly, then wrap in cling film and leave to rest.
2. Grease and line two baking sheets.
3. Cut the onions in half and slice, then cook slowly in a frying pan with the butter. When the onions are translucent add the sugar, garlic and balsamic vinegar and continue to cook until soft.
4. Add the apples to the pan and cook for a few minutes until coated in all the juices and softened. Allow to cool.
5. Roll out the pastry on a floured surface until 3mm thick. Using an 11cm pastry cutter cut out approximately 12 discs.
6. Add the crumbled cheese to the onion mix and season with salt and pepper to taste.
7. Spoon a tbsp of the mixture in the centre of the pastry disk, brush the edges with beaten egg and fold the pastry over to form a crescent shape. Pinch the pastry together and brush with egg and place on a prepared baking sheet. Leave the pasties to rest for 45 mins before baking in the oven at 180C/160C Fan/Gas Mark 4 for 15 minutes.

CARR'S FLOUR

30 SUNDAY

1 MONDAY

2 TUESDAY

3 WEDNESDAY

4 THURSDAY

5 FRIDAY

6 SATURDAY

On this week...

July 1st 1972

TAKING A STAND

The first official UK Gay Pride Rally was held in London. The date was chosen as the nearest Saturday to the anniversary of the Stonewall riots of 1969. Around 1,000 people marched from Hyde Park to Trafalgar Square, chanting 'Gay is good'. Rights campaigner Peter Tatchell admitted protesters were openly abused by bystanders.

Marches and rallies continued in London every summer up until 1981, when Pride moved to Huddersfield in support of the queer community's protest against West Yorkshire Police, who were repeatedly raiding a well-known gay club. By the 1990s Pride was taking place over several weeks, with events, concerts and other large gatherings, as well as the march and rally. In 1992, London was selected to hold the first ever Europride, with attendance estimated at 100,000.

For 1996, the event was renamed 'Lesbian, Gay, Bisexual and Transgender Pride' and became the largest free music festival in Europe.

Fun anagram!
Change handouts into a number

Answer: Thousand

Money-saving tip

When you're on holiday, remember you can claim back tax on in-store purchases in Europe (if you're a UK resident) with a minimum spend. In France, for example, you must spend €100 per purchase or shop, which saves around €16.

Mood boosters

Set yourself a goal for today! It doesn't have to be anything ambitious – maybe going for a brisk walk or catching up with a friend you've not seen in ages. Make your goal specific, give yourself a time frame to achieve it and make it manageable. The sense of achieving it will give you a lift!

A PHOTO TO TREASURE

When I am melting in a rare British heatwave, I would love to be back in Spain where this photo of me was taken in the Seventies. We had wonderful family holidays there and my sons, now grown up, still talk about them. Happy days!

Chris Tait, via email

Recipe of the week

BAKEWELL TART TRAYBAKE

SERVES: **15** PREP: **10 mins** COOK: **45 mins**

150g (5oz) plain flour
150g (5oz) caster sugar, split into 50g (1½oz) and 100g (3½oz)
200g (7oz) unsalted butter, softened, divided in two
150g (5oz) ground almonds
1 egg
200g (7oz) raspberry jam
Handful of flaked almonds
Icing sugar to dust

1. Preheat the oven to 180C/165C Fan/Gas Mark 4.
2. Put the flour and 50g (1½oz) of the caster sugar in a mixing bowl before rubbing in 100g (3½oz) of butter with your fingertips. When the mixture resembles crumbs, pour it into the lined traybake tin, spread it evenly and press it down so the crumbs loosely join together. Bake the base for 15 mins.
3. While the base is baking, combine the remaining 100g (3½oz) of butter, 100g (3½oz) of sugar, the ground almonds and the egg in a mixing bowl with a spoon to make the frangipane topping.
4. When the base has had its 15 mins, remove it from the oven and add the jam, spreading it with the back of the spoon to make an even layer over the top, followed by all of the frangipane mix (this will be a thicker layer) and a sprinkling of flaked almonds before returning to the oven for a further 30 mins.
5. Once golden on top, remove from the oven and allow to cool completely before removing from the tin. Dust with icing sugar, slice into bars and top with flaked almonds.

EASY PEASY BAKING CAMPAIGN

7 SUNDAY

8 MONDAY

9 TUESDAY

10 WEDNESDAY

11 THURSDAY

12 FRIDAY

13 SATURDAY

On this week...

July 9th 1982

THE QUEEN'S VISITOR

Around 7.15am, the Queen awoke to find a barefoot intruder, Michael Fagan, sat on the edge of her bed, clutching a broken ashtray. While the armed policeman outside the royal bedroom went off duty early to walk the dogs, Fagan had shimmied up the drainpipes and climbed into the Queen's apartments. It was only when Fagan asked for a cigarette that she was able to quietly raise the alarm, under the pretext of sending for a servant.

However, thinking the bell was faulty, the Buckingham Palace policeman dismissed these alarms, leaving the Queen calmly talking away to Fagan in her nightie for ten more minutes. At last, help arrived from the maid and duty footman and Fagan was arrested, but not charged for trespassing in the Queen's bedroom since it was then a civil offence and proceedings would have compromised the Queen's position as head of state.

This was the sixth breach of security at the Queen's London residence in recent months.

Fun anagram!
Change **danger** into a place where you grow flowers

Answer: Garden

Money-saving tip

If you need a new tablet, laptop or mobile phone, buying refurbished can significantly cut the cost. These are devices that have been sent back by customers and then restored to full working order. They usually come with a guarantee – see musicmagpie.co.uk or mobile.co.uk.

Mood boosters

Stand tall and be proud! Studies have shown that having a confident stance gives you a more positive outlook on life. How you carry yourself influences how you feel, so stand straight, pull your shoulders back and lift your head up slightly – your new stance will help you shine!

A PHOTO TO TREASURE

This photo of me (on the right) with my father and my brother James was taken on Teignmouth pier in 1946. We travelled there from our home in Exeter by train. Generations of my family, including my children and grandchildren, have visited Teignmouth, where I now live.

David Lee, Devon

Recipe of the week

BASIL PESTO, PEA AND GOAT'S CHEESE RISOTTO

SERVES: **2** PREP: **10 mins** COOK: **25 mins**

1 tbsp Lunaio extra virgin olive oil
200g Seggiano Arborio Risotto Rice
700ml vegetable stock
100g frozen peas
5 tbsp Seggiano Raw Basil Pesto
60g soft goat's cheese
Lunaio lemon oil, to serve

1. Heat the olive oil in a large flat-bottomed pan over a medium/low heat then add the rice. Stir to coat the grains in oil and toast for 2-3 mins, stirring continuously until the rice is slightly translucent.
2. Add the stock a ladleful at a time, and simmer gently until the liquid has been absorbed before adding more, stirring frequently. Cook until the rice is al dente.
3. Meanwhile, tip the peas into a bowl or jug and cover with boiling water. Once defrosted, drain the water then stir the peas into the risotto. Cook for a further 5 mins or until the rice is tender.
4. Remove from the heat and stir through 4 tbsp basil pesto and half of the goat's cheese.
5. Divide between 2 serving bowls, swirl through the remaining pesto and goat's cheese and finish with a drizzle of lemon oil.

SEGGIANO

14 SUNDAY

15 MONDAY

16 TUESDAY

17 WEDNESDAY

18 THURSDAY

19 FRIDAY

20 SATURDAY

On this week...

July 19th 1952

PHOTO 'FINNISH'!

The opening ceremony took place for the 15th modern Olympiad in the Finnish capital, Helsinki. It was rainy and the Olympic stadium had no roof, but 70,435 spectators watched the inaugural march featuring a record 5,469 people. There were 4,955 athletes from 69 nations taking part, including delegations from Israel and the Soviet Union for the first time. The Soviet gymnasts proved impressive: Viktor Chukarin won four golds, and the women won the team competition, beginning a streak that would continue for 40 years.

One of the biggest heroes of the Games was Czechoslovakian runner Emil Zátopek (above), who won the 5,000m, defended his 10,000m title, and then took his third gold medal in his first-ever marathon to complete a triple that remains unique in Olympic history.

The US secured the most medals: 40 gold, 19 silver and 17 bronze, while the host country won six gold, three silver and 13 bronze.

Fun anagram!

Change **dear** into something you do with a book

Answer: Read

Money-saving tip

When flying on holiday, you can ask for hot water on the plane. If you take along your own preferred tea bags, coffee, soup or instant noodles, you'll save on the cost of expensive drinks and food on board (and will get a better cuppa too!).

Mood boosters

Make your summer holiday one where your wellness takes priority. Whether that's a fitness break in Cornwall, a one-day relaxation retreat in the countryside or a group walking trip to the seaside, focusing on your exercise and nutrition can boost your physical and mental health.

A PHOTO TO TREASURE

These are my granddaughters when we took them on a day trip to Scarborough. Charlotte decided that this is the way you walk along the prom and Emma (aged three) copied her sister. I thought they looked so cute. They are both in their 30s now with families of their own.

Elaine McGuigan, Pudsey

Recipe of the week

CHIMICHURRI EGG, POTATO AND GREENS SALAD

SERVES: **6** PREP: **10 mins** COOK: **20 mins**

500g (1lb 2oz) new potatoes, halved if large
100g (4oz) green beans, trimmed
100g (4oz) frozen peas
6 medium British Lion quality eggs
3 tbsp capers (optional)
1 sweet Romaine lettuce, washed and trimmed
Chimichurri dressing:
4 tbsp fresh coriander leaves
4 tbsp fresh flat parsley leaves
1 clove garlic
1 tsp dried oregano
½ tsp dried chilli flakes
6 tbsp olive oil
2 tbsp red wine vinegar
Salt and ground black pepper

1. Cook the potatoes in a pan of boiling salted water for 10-15 mins. Drain, rinse then set aside to cool in a bowl.
2. Refill the pan with boiling water, add the green beans and boil for 3 mins, then add the peas and bring back to the boil. Drain, rinse in cold water then leave to drain.
3. While the vegetables cook, put the eggs in a small pan and cover with cold water. Bring to the boil, then simmer uncovered for 5 mins (water bubbling).
4. Drain the eggs and run them under cold water, tapping the shells as they cool. Once cold enough to handle, peel and discard the shells. Cut the eggs in half and leave to cool.
5. Next make the dressing. Place all the ingredients in a large jug and mix with a fork or small whisk until a smooth dressing forms. Pour over the potatoes, add the cooked vegetables and capers and mix well.
6. Arrange the salad leaves in a large salad bowl, heap the vegetables into the centre, then arrange the eggs on top. Serve chilled.

BRITISH LION EGGS

21 SUNDAY

22 MONDAY

23 TUESDAY

24 WEDNESDAY

25 THURSDAY

26 FRIDAY

27 SATURDAY

On this week...

July 26th 1952

THE END OF EVITA

Eva Duarte de Peron, wife of the Argentine President General Juan Domingo Peron, died from cancer, aged 33. Argentina's most famous first lady was greatly loved by the people and had recently been proclaimed 'spiritual chief of the Argentine nation'. July 26th was immediately declared a National Day of Mourning.

Born into a poor family, Eva had moved to Buenos Aires to pursue a career in the theatre. She met Peron in 1944 when he was Vice President and the couple married a year later.

When General Peron became President, Eva devoted her time to the poor. She was a champion of the working classes, spending millions of pounds of public money to improve their lives and organising mass political rallies to give them more political power. She also fought for women to be able to vote and campaigned to legalise divorce.

Fun anagram!
Change genre into a colour

Answer: Green

Money-saving tip

Discover when your local supermarket adds its yellow discount stickers by experimenting with the timing of your visits. You'll often get the biggest discounts last thing on a Sunday afternoon or just before a big holiday. Certain supermarkets discount heavily on a Monday.

Mood boosters

Put away your phone today! Frequent mobile use is associated with reduced happiness, according to research. It's thought that seeing everyone else's social calendars can make it difficult to stay present in your own life, plus keeping on top of news can increase stress levels. Instead, spend today in *your* moment.

A PHOTO TO TREASURE

My dad, Roy Thickpenny, had a great sense of adventure and we went on many family camping trips in the Seventies and Eighties. The tent always leaked and the car always broke down but the memories never fade. This is me with my brother, Rob.

Rachel Hawkins, via email

Recipe of the week

GIN AND TONIC DRIZZLE LOAF

MAKES: **1 loaf** PREP: **15 mins** COOK: **45 mins**

1 grapefruit/orange or 2 lemons/limes
175g (6oz) self-raising flour
175g (6oz) caster sugar + 75g (2½oz) for soaking syrup
175g (6oz) unsalted butter, softened
3 eggs
120ml (4fl oz) gin split into 50ml (1½fl oz) and 70ml (2½fl oz)
75ml (3fl oz) tonic water
150g (5oz) icing sugar

1. Preheat the oven to 180C/165C Fan/Gas Mark 4. Take whichever citrus you are using and cut half into slices for decorating. Zest and juice the other half.
2. In a bowl, combine the flour, citrus zest and 175g (6oz) of caster sugar. Add the butter, eggs, 50ml (1½fl oz) gin, 2 tbsp of citrus juice and whisk until smooth.
3. Pour the batter into a lined loaf tin and bake for 35 mins. Remove and leave to cool.
4. Pour the remaining citrus juice, tonic and 75g (2½oz) sugar into a saucepan and heat for 5-8 mins until the sugar has dissolved. Allow to cool slightly then stir in the remaining gin (70ml/2½fl oz). Set aside 3 tbsp of the syrup.
5. Poke the loaf all over with a fork and drizzle with the syrup from the saucepan.
6. When the loaf is completely cool, remove from the tin. Combine the 3 tbsp of reserved syrup with the icing sugar to make a glaze and pour over the top of your loaf, slightly pushing it down the sides with the end of a spoon to create a drip effect. Decorate with citrus slices and serve.

EASY PEASY BAKING CAMPAIGN BY UK FLOUR MILLERS

28 SUNDAY

29 MONDAY

30 TUESDAY

31 WEDNESDAY

1 THURSDAY

2 FRIDAY

3 SATURDAY

On this week...

July 29th 1965

I NEED SOMEBODY!

The Beatles movie Help! had its Royal World Premiere at the London Pavilion in the West End, attended by Princess Margaret and the Earl of Snowdon. Sadly, the Beatles' second big screen offering was not received with the same high level of admiration as their first film, A Hard Day's Night. However, Help! is now credited with influencing the development of music videos.

According to interviews conducted with Paul McCartney, George Harrison and Ringo Starr, director Richard Lester was given a larger budget for this film than he had for A Hard Day's Night, thanks to the commercial success of the latter. Thus, this feature film was in colour and shot on overseas locations.

The Beatles didn't enjoy filming Help!, nor were they pleased with the end product. In 1970, John Lennon said they felt like extras in their own film: "The film was out of our control. With A Hard Day's Night we had a lot of input and it was semi-realistic. But with Help!, Dick Lester didn't tell us what it was all about."

Fun anagram!
Change **shore** into an animal

Answer: Horse

Money-saving tip

If your dishwasher is around 10 years old, or more, it may be causing high energy bills plus will be less environmentally friendly than newer models. If you're looking to upgrade, chose one with an A+++ rating. Choosing an eco-friendly dishwasher can save you around £270 over the lifetime of the appliance.

Mood boosters

Essential oils can be used to boost your energy levels and your mood. Basil, rosemary, grapefruit, lime and bergamot have all been shown to energise – and you can fill your house with them with the likes of diffusers, room mists and candles, or use a rollerball on your pulse points for an instant lift.

A PHOTO TO TREASURE

I think this holiday photo was taken around 1926. It shows my mum, Lily, balanced between my dad, Stan (on the right), and my Uncle Percy. My dad was a smoker who died in 1940 when he was 33 and I was just a year old.

Stanley Dart, via email

Recipe of the week

SALMON, WATERCRESS AND PEA QUICHE

SERVES: **8** PREP: **15 mins** COOK: **20 mins**

1 (375g/13oz) pack ready to roll shortcrust pastry
2 tbsp olive oil
1 large onion, sliced
1 (80g/3oz) bag watercress
150g (5oz) frozen peas
2 tsp wholegrain or Dijon mustard
1 (212g/7oz) can wild pink salmon
4 medium British Lion eggs
200ml (7fl oz) whole milk
Salt and ground black pepper

1. Preheat the oven to 220C/200C Fan/Gas Mark 7. Unroll the pastry and use to line a 28 x 21 x 3cm deep rectangular tin, trimming the edges and pushing them into the base to fit.
2. Lightly prick the base all over and, using baking paper, cover with baking beans and bake for 15 mins.
3. Heat the oil in a frying pan, add the onions and a pinch of salt and cook over a medium heat for 5 mins.
4. Save a handful of watercress leaves for the garnish; roughly chop the rest and stir into the onions along with the frozen peas. Cook until the leaves have wilted. Remove from the heat, stir in the mustard and season to taste.
5. Drain the salmon, discard any skin and large bones then flake the rest.
6. Remove the pastry from the oven and lift out the paper and beans. Scatter half the filling over the base, and the salmon, followed by the rest of the vegetables.
7. Beat the eggs with the milk then pour into the pastry case. Bake for 25 mins until the filling is golden and set. Cool before scattering with the reserved watercress. Serve warm or cold.

BRITISH LION EGGS

4 SUNDAY

5 MONDAY

6 TUESDAY

7 WEDNESDAY

8 THURSDAY

9 FRIDAY

10 SATURDAY

On this week...

August 9th 1972

WEST END MESSIAH

The Tim Rice and Andrew Lloyd Webber musical Jesus Christ Superstar made its West End debut at the Palace Theatre. Following a hugely successful concept album and Broadway run, the rock opera came to London with Paul Nicholas as Jesus of Nazareth. Loosely based on the Gospels' accounts of the Passion, much of the story focused on Judas, played by Stephen Tate.

The show proved highly controversial with some religious groups who considered it blasphemous. Demonstrators from the National Secular Society protested outside the theatre on the opening night singing hymns and handing out leaflets. At the same time, some Jews claimed it bolstered the anti-Semitic belief that the Jews were responsible for Jesus' death and that most of the villains are Jewish. Nevertheless, by 1980 the musical had grossed $237 million worldwide and ran for over eight years, becoming the longest-running West End musical before being taken over by Cats in 1989.

Fun anagram!
Change pagers into a fruit

Answer: Grapes

Money-saving tip

When online shopping, avoid getting sucked in to buying more items in order to get free delivery if you spend over a certain amount. Free gifts or free delivery can motivate you to buy more – step away for a while and, when you return, you'll be less motivated to buy.

Mood boosters

While we can't all enjoy wild swimming, we can get its benefits – boosting your immunity and increasing your dopamine levels, which boosts your mood – by taking a daily cold shower. A short burst can really make a difference – start in a warm shower then see if you can go cold for 10 seconds, then 20, then 30!

A PHOTO TO TREASURE

This is the only photo I have of me with my dear mum. It was taken in 1969 when I had recently left school and we went for a week in Morecambe before I started work. In those days I used to buy my clothes from Etam and Chelsea Girl.

Sylvia Foster, via email

Recipe of the week

STRAWBERRY AND CHAMPAGNE SHORTBREAD

MAKES: **20** PREP: **25 mins** COOK: **25 mins**

225g (8oz) unsalted butter (plus extra for greasing tray)
100g (4oz) caster sugar
½ tsp salt
2 tbsp strawberry jam
285g (10oz) Carr's Plain Flour (plus extra for dusting)
200g (7oz) icing sugar
2 tbsp Champagne
¾ tbsp strawberry jam
Cold water

1. Preheat the oven to 170C/150C Fan/Gas Mark 3.
2. Cream together the butter, sugar, salt and jam in a large bowl until light and fluffy.
3. Add the flour a little at a time, until mixed in.
4. Be careful not to over work the ingredients.
5. Once the dough has formed, wrap in cling film and place in the fridge for 2 hours or until cool.
6. Sprinkle some flour onto your work surface and knead lightly until you have a loose dough.
7. Roll out the dough until it's roughly 0.5cm thick.
8. Cut out using a cutter and place onto a lightly greased baking tray and bake for 25 mins (until pale brown and crisp).
9. Allow to cool on a wire rack.
10. Meanwhile, stir together the icing sugar, champagne and jam in a small bowl and mix until a stiff paste has formed. Add more champagne or water to loosen if needed. Dip each biscuit until half covered.
11. Place back onto a wire rack until dry, then enjoy with the rest of the champagne!

CARR'S FLOUR

11 SUNDAY

12 MONDAY

13 TUESDAY

14 WEDNESDAY

15 THURSDAY

16 FRIDAY

17 SATURDAY

On this week...

August 13th 1967

A BOX OFFICE HIT

The film Bonnie and Clyde, released in 1967, pioneered a new era of filmmaking, tearing down barriers in the depiction of violence and sexuality. The movie was based on the Great Depression-era robbery team. Clyde Barrow (played by Warren Beatty) turns a chance encounter with bored, small-town Bonnie Parker (Faye Dunaway) into the opportunity to launch a crime spree. The lovers team up with Clyde's brother Buck (Gene Hackman), his timid wife, Blanche, and a dim-witted henchman, C.W. Moss. The gang thwarts police efforts to capture them, until a fateful encounter on a country road.

The film glamorised crime in a way that would have been unthinkable under the censorship guidelines known as the Hays Production Code, which had been superseded by a ratings system in 1966. Critics feared the film would unleash a tidal wave of cinematic carnage, while its defenders predicted it would free filmmakers from the corporate chains that had previously stifled artistic creativity.

Fun anagram!
Change **nails** into a slow animal

Answer: Snail

Money-saving tip

You'd be surprised at how many energy guzzling gadgets you leave switched on overnight (such as your TV, washing machine and phone charger). Do a quick check of the house before bed and watch your energy usage fall.

Mood boosters

Kickstart your mornings by opening your curtains first thing. Spend a few moments by the window, allowing the daylight in. Daylight helps control your body clock and the light encourages the production of energy-boosting hormones such as cortisol. Consider investing in a daylight alarm clock for dark winters.

A PHOTO TO TREASURE

This photo, taken in 1956, means more to me than ever now.
I was 15 and my boyfriend, Brian, was 20. We were on the beach at Sandown on the Isle of Wight. We were married in 1958 and had 64 years together before Brian passed away.
  Valerie Temple, Essex

Recipe of the week

BEEF AND KALE LASAGNE

SERVES: **4** PREP: **20 mins** COOK: **35 mins**

1 onion, chopped
500g (18oz) extra lean minced beef
1 tsp dried mixed herbs
400g (14oz) can chopped tomatoes
½ x 200g (7oz) bag ready-prepared kale
6 lasagne sheets
350g (12oz) tub cheese sauce
50g (2oz) Cheddar cheese, grated

1. Preheat the oven to 200C/180C Fan/Gas Mark 6.
2. Fry the onion, beef and herbs for 5 mins. Add the tomatoes and cover and cook for 10 mins, adding the kale for the last 3 mins.
3. Place 2 sheets of lasagne in an ovenproof dish, top with half the mince. Place 2 sheets of lasagne on top then the remaining mince. Add the final 2 sheets of lasagne. Pour over the cheese sauce and sprinkle over the cheese.
4. Bake for 30-35 mins until golden. Serve with a fresh green salad.
DISCOVER GREAT VEG

18 SUNDAY

19 MONDAY

20 TUESDAY

21 WEDNESDAY

22 THURSDAY

23 FRIDAY

24 SATURDAY

On this week...

August 18th 1969

A LEGENDARY MISHAP

Over 50 years ago, Rolling Stones frontman Mick Jagger was accidentally shot while filming the movie Ned Kelly.

In one of Ned Kelly's final scenes, filmed on August 18th 1969, Jagger says he was tasked with "shooting a lot of policemen". He was given a pistol loaded with blanks, and he filmed the scene as scripted. However, the pistol backfired, causing a slew of shrapnel to lodge itself deep into Jagger's hand, and he was promptly taken to a Canberra hospital for treatment.

With his music career potentially on the line following the injury, Jagger spent hours playing guitar and trying to rehabilitate his severely injured hand.

Thankfully his hand did heal and the incident even led to the birth of one of the band's most popular songs. Whilst recovering, Jagger wrote the song Brown Sugar, inspired by the accident.

Fun anagram!

Change **panel** into a mode of transport

Answer: Plane

Money-saving tip

You won't be able to tell the difference between LED lights and "normal" ones as they now give instant light, but you will make savings! Swapping regular light bulbs for energy-saving options can save up to £55 a year.

Mood boosters

We often experience a post-lunch lethargic slump, which can affect our mood. Give yourself an afternoon pick-me-up by making or buying a vegetable juice. Try a blend of beetroot, apple and ginger for a hit of energising vitamins and minerals.

A PHOTO TO TREASURE

Here are my mum and dad, Edna and Derek, on their wedding day in August 1952 when they were both 21. They honeymooned in Llandudno and returned home with just ten shillings (50p) in their pocket. My dad was able to celebrate their diamond wedding anniversary shortly before he passed away.

Sue Dean, King's Swinford

Recipe of the week

PISTACHIO AND WHITE CHOCOLATE ICE CREAM SANDWICHES

MAKES: **6** PREP: **10 mins** COOK: **15 mins**

120g (4oz) unsalted butter
225g (8oz) light brown sugar
1 egg
300g (11oz) plain flour
½ tsp bicarbonate of soda
¼ tsp salt
300g (11oz) white chocolate, roughly chopped
100g (4oz) pistachios, roughly chopped
Tub vanilla ice cream

1. Preheat the oven to 180C/165C Fan/Gas Mark 4.
2. In a large mixing bowl, cream together the butter and sugar with an electric hand whisk.
3. Add the egg and mix until combined, before adding the flour, bicarbonate and salt. Mix well with your hands. When the dough starts to come together, add 150g (5oz) chopped white chocolate and 50g (2oz) of chopped pistachios. Bring together to form a ball of dough.
4. Roll the dough into 12 evenly sized balls and place on the lined baking tray, 6 at a time as the cookies need space to spread as they bake.
5. Bake in the oven for 7 mins, turn the tray and bake for a further 7 mins then allow the cookies to cool. Repeat with the rest of the cookie dough balls.
6. When the cookies are cool, sandwich two together with a generous scoop of ice cream and decorate as you wish – melt the remaining white chocolate in the microwave in 10 second increments (stirring between each to be careful that it doesn't burn) and dip them, roll them in the remaining chopped pistachios... do both or leave plain!

EASY PEASY BAKING CAMPAIGN

25 SUNDAY

26 MONDAY

27 TUESDAY

28 WEDNESDAY

29 THURSDAY

30 FRIDAY

31 SATURDAY

On this week...

August 26th 1959

THE BIRTH OF A BRITISH ICON

Sixty five years ago the British Motor Corporation introduced the Morris Mini-Minor. The original design broke the mould and revolutionised the motor industry. Designed by Alec Issigonis, the car was only 10ft long but seated four passengers. It changed the way we looked at small cars and sent automotive designers back to the drawing board.

It was to become the best-selling British car in history, with more than 5.3 million units sold over a 41-year production run.

No other car has come close to achieving those figures. The Mini was simple, stylish and self-confident. Its clever use of space, compact design and excellent road handling ensured it was to become a fun, affordable and perennial classic icon.

Fun anagram!

Change raptor into a talkative animal

Answer: Parrot

Money-saving tip

Look at online retailer Approved Food, which sells surplus and short-dated products at a discount. Also sign up to Olio and Too Good To Go, plus Morrison's magic bags where it's possible to get £10 of food for a third of the price.

Mood boosters

A power nap can pep you up! Try to nap between 2pm and 4pm – any later will affect your night's sleep. Don't worry if you don't really feel like you're napping, after a few days' practise you'll notice your thoughts drop to a more restful level. Sleep for no more than 30 minutes to avoid feeling groggy.

A PHOTO TO TREASURE

I just adore this photo of my dad, Peter, when he was a toddler. Taken sometime around 1947, it shows him walking along the promenade holding hands with his gran on the right and his Aunty Lil. I think he looks so sweet in his little outfit.

Nicola Richardson, via email

Recipe of the week

MANDARIN JAM AND RHUBARB CAKE

SERVES: **8-10**   PREP: **15 mins**   COOK: **50 mins**

150g (5oz) unsalted butter, softened
150g (5oz) caster sugar
3 eggs
150g (5oz) self-raising flour
1 tsp baking powder
200g (7oz) rhubarb, chopped
4 tbsp Seggiano Mandarin Jam
Icing sugar, to dust

1. Preheat the oven to 180C/160C Fan/Gas Mark 4. Grease and line a 20cm round cake tin.
2. In a large bowl, cream together the butter and sugar until light and fluffy.
3. Beat in the eggs, one at a time, until well combined.
4. Sift in the flour and baking powder and fold into the mixture until smooth.
5. Fold in the chopped rhubarb.
6. Spoon half of the mixture into the prepared tin and smooth the top.
7. Spoon over the mandarin jam, spreading it out evenly.
8. Spoon the remaining cake mixture over the jam and smooth the top.
9. Bake in the preheated oven for 45-50 mins, or until a skewer inserted into the center comes out clean.
10. Remove the cake from the oven and leave to cool in the tin for 10 mins, before turning out onto a wire rack to cool completely.
11. Dust the top with icing sugar before serving.

SEGGIANO

1 SUNDAY

2 MONDAY

3 TUESDAY

4 WEDNESDAY

5 THURSDAY

6 FRIDAY

7 SATURDAY

On this week...

September 6th 1962

HISTORIC DISCOVERY

The first of the 'Blackfriars Ships' was discovered by archaeologist Peter Marsden in mud under Blackfriars Bridge on the River Thames. From pottery shards in the wreckage, Marsden estimated the ship sank during the 2nd century AD, when Britain was ruled by the Roman Empire. The wreck was discovered while building a riverside embankment wall along the River Thames. Marsden discovered the first on 6th September 1962, then went on to discover another two 'ships' in 1970. A later discovery added to the previous three wrecks, constituting now what is known as the four Blackfriars wrecks.

Fun anagram!

Change **melon** into another fruit

Answer: Lemon

Money-saving tip

A little careful planning in the kitchen can save you money. Batch cooking could save you £158 over a year while using the right-sized pan with a lid can save £72. Filling your kettle with the right amount of water could save you £19 per year.

Mood boosters

Exercise is vital for energy production as it gets the oxygen whizzing around your body, giving every cell a vitality boost. Do whatever feels good to wake up your body – stretching your arms up towards the sky, swinging your arms from side to side, stretching your quads or slowly bending forward to try to touch your toes.

A PHOTO TO TREASURE

This is a photo of my late mum at the seaside. It would have been taken when she was a young lady and her clothes and shoes would have been very fashionable at that time. So elegant! I love them and wish I had them now.
Heather McEwen, Norwich

Recipe of the week

CALIFORNIA WALNUT MINCE CHILLI

SERVES: **5** PREP: **10 mins** COOK: **15 mins**

100g (3½oz) California Walnuts
300g (11oz) mushrooms
1 tbsp oil
2 cloves garlic, crushed
1 tsp ground cumin
1 tsp chilli powder
400g (14oz) can chopped tomatoes
2 tbsp tomato puree
400g (14oz) can red kidney beans, drained and rinsed
400g (14oz) can black beans, drained and rinsed
2 tbsp chopped coriander

1. Place the walnuts in a food processor and mix to give a coarse crumb. Repeat with the mushrooms and mix into the walnuts.
2. Heat the oil in a large saucepan and fry the walnut mixture and garlic for 5 mins. Add the spices and cook for 1 min.
3. Stir in the tomatoes, tomato puree and both beans and cook gently for 10 mins, stirring occasionally. Season and stir in the coriander.

CALIFORNIA WALNUTS

8 SUNDAY

9 MONDAY

10 TUESDAY

11 WEDNESDAY

12 THURSDAY

13 FRIDAY

14 SATURDAY

On this week...

September 14th 1982

DEATH OF A PRINCESS

Princess Grace of Monaco was driving with her youngest daughter, Stephanie, near Monte Carlo when she reportedly suffered a stroke and lost control of her car, which plunged down a mountainside.

Seventeen-year-old Stephanie survived, but Princess Grace died the following day. Her husband, Prince Rainier, and the couple's children were at the former Hollywood star's bedside when she died following a brain haemorrhage.

On the day of her funeral, she was mourned by Nancy Reagan, Princess Diana and Cary Grant at the Monaco Cathedral during a 75-minute service watched by approximately 100 million people.

Fun anagram!

Change **resist** into a member of the family

Answer: Sister

Money-saving tip

When selling unwanted items online for extra cash, be specific with your wording to maximise sales. Shoes labelled 'sneaker' fetch £32 on average, compared to £21 for those labelled 'trainer'. Perfumes described as 'authentic' sell for £13 more on average than those described as 'genuine'.

Mood boosters

Doodling has proven therapeutic effects and is a simple yet powerful way to boost your mood. Focus on what you're drawing – let all other thoughts go – and draw what makes you feel happy, be it a sunset, animal or tree. Adult colouring books are also great mood lifters.

A PHOTO TO TREASURE

This photo of me (on the left) with my cousin, Marion, was taken at the Rockefeller Centre in New York. The date was September 9th 2018 and the next day we had the memorable experience of visiting Ground Zero, where we saw the Survivor Tree that had been saved from the wreckage of 9/11.

Rhianydd Garrod, via email

Recipe of the week

GREEK STYLE SPINACH, FETA AND EGG TARTS

SERVES: **6** PREP: **10 mins** COOK: **20-25 mins**

500g (18oz) frozen whole baby leaf spinach
2 tbsp olive oil
1 bunch spring onions, trimmed and sliced
1 clove garlic
50g (2oz) pitted green olives, chopped
100g feta cheese, crumbled
Grated nutmeg to taste
Salt and ground black pepper
1 (320g/11oz) sheet of puff pastry
7 medium British Lion quality eggs

1. Heat a frying pan, add the spinach and cook from frozen, stirring until the spinach has thawed. Spoon into a sieve and press out any excess moisture.
2. Heat the oil, add the onions and garlic and fry for a min. Remove from the heat and stir in the spinach, olives and feta. Mix well then season (with nutmeg too).
3. Preheat the oven to 220C/200C Fan/Gas Mark 7. Unroll the pastry and cut into 6 evenly sized pieces and place on a large baking paper lined tray. Beat one of the eggs in a small bowl, then brush 2cm of the edges of the pastry with egg. Prick the centre of the pastry with a fork.
4. Stir the rest of the beaten egg into the spinach mixture, then divide between the pastry pieces. Use a fork and spoon to spread it up to the egg-washed border, then make a hollow in the centre of the spinach mix. Crack an egg into the middle of each.
5. Bake in the centre of the oven for 15-20 mins or until the pastry is golden and the eggs set. Serve warm with a tomato, mint and cucumber salad.

BRITISH LION EGGS

15 SUNDAY

16 MONDAY

17 TUESDAY

18 WEDNESDAY

19 THURSDAY

20 FRIDAY

21 SATURDAY

On this week...

September 17th 1972

HAWKEYE AND HOT LIPS

Viewers in America were treated to their first episode of M*A*S*H, the comedy drama set in a mobile army surgical hospital during the Korean War. We took their ensemble cast characters to our hearts, from wise-cracking Hawkeye Pierce (Alan Alda) and Trapper John (Wayne Rogers) to long-suffering Commander Henry Blake (McLean Stevenson), pugnacious Frank Burns (Larry Linville) and Hot Lips Houlihan (Loretta Swit). The show perfectly blended quirky and irreverent humour with touching poignant moments.

The unusual setting enabled the writers to tackle difficult subjects such as bereavement, loneliness and mental health issues with great sensitivity. When M*A*S*H finally ended in 1983 after 12 years and 251 episodes, the finale – Goodbye, Farewell and Amen – became the most-watched and highest-rated single episode in US TV history at the time, with a record-breaking 125m viewers.

Fun anagram!

Change finder into a person you need to be happy

Answer: Friend

Money-saving tip

For a delicious breakfast that doesn't require any energy use of a toaster, microwave or hob, choose overnight oats. Pop oats, yoghurt, grated apple or whatever fruit and flavouring you like into a mason jar before going to bed and you'll have an instant treat in the morning.

Mood boosters

For an instant blast of energy, try tapping the top centre of your chest just below your collar bone. Use your fingertips and tap for 20 seconds. It's thought to stimulate your thymus gland, encouraging the production of immune-boosting T cells, relieving stress and giving energy levels a lift.

A PHOTO TO TREASURE

Here I am, aged 11, with my first bicycle. It was a longed-for birthday present. Up until then I had been given clothes and was disappointed the previous year to receive a bright blue Harris Tweed jacket. I wasted no time in showing my bicycle off to my friends.
Timothy Hertslet, Portsmouth

Recipe of the week

JAM & CUSTARD TART

MAKES: **1 tart** PREP: **30 mins** COOK: **45 mins**

300g (10½oz) plain flour
3 tbsp caster sugar + 40g (1½oz) for custard
150g (5oz) unsalted butter
3 tbsp cold water
40g (1½oz) custard powder
450ml (¾ pt) milk
½ jar Bonne Maman Strawberry Jam
Icing sugar

1. Preheat the oven to 200C/180C Fan/Gas Mark 6. In a bowl, rub together the flour, 3 tbsp sugar and butter. Add in the water and bring together to form a dough.
2. Tip the dough out onto a lightly floured work surface and cut off a third. Set it to one side.
3. Roll the dough out, big enough to line your tart tin, drape it over the tin, folding and pushing the pastry into the corners. Leave any excess to hang over the edge. Prick the base all over with a knife.
4. Roll out the remaining third of dough, and cut out some stars, placing them on a lined baking tray.
5. Place both the tart case and stars in the oven and bake for 20-25 mins until lightly golden.
6. Once the case is baked, make your custard filling by whisking together the custard powder with 40g (1½oz) sugar and a splash of milk to form a paste. When there are no lumps, add the remaining milk and place over a medium heat. Whisk until a thick custard. Pour into the tart case, spread and allow to cool to room temperature before placing in the fridge to cool further.
7. Spread the jam over the top and pop back in the oven for 15-20 mins until the jam just begins to bubble.
8. Allow the tart to cool slightly before placing the pastry stars on top, dusting with icing sugar and serving.

EASY PEASY BAKING CAMPAIGN WITH BONNE MAMAN

22 SUNDAY

23 MONDAY

24 TUESDAY

25 WEDNESDAY

26 THURSDAY

27 FRIDAY

28 SATURDAY

On this week...

September 23rd 1972

CRAZEE FOR SLADE

Wolverhampton's favourite rockers Slade achieved their third week at No.1 in the charts with Mama Weer All Crazee Now. The song was the first single released from their third studio album, Slayed? and spent ten weeks in the charts.

Songwriter Jim Lea was inspired to write the catchy tune after being at a Chuck Berry concert earlier that year, where he noticed how Berry kept stopping to let the crowd sing along. "It was amazing," Lea said. "I thought, 'why not write the crowd into the songs?', and so... all the chants were written into the tunes."

Slade went on to become one of the most successful British bands of the Seventies, dominating the UK charts with 17 consecutive top 20 hits and six No.1s. In 1973 their final No.1 single, Merry Xmas Everybody, sold more than 1 million copies globally. Noddy Holder has been known to describe the song as his pension scheme as it still generates around £500,000 a year in royalties!

Fun anagram!

Change teach into something you mustn't do at school

Answer: Cheat

Money-saving tip

Save on vet expenses by keeping your pet up-to-date with parasite prevention, yearly vaccinations and ensure it's a healthy weight so is less likely to become ill. For cats and dogs, brushing teeth early can help prevent dental disease setting in.

Mood boosters

Mess saps your energy because your brain doesn't know where to focus its attention, say scientists. A major clearout can seem daunting so instead break it down – take five minutes to organise your coffee table or kitchen counter and you'll find your mind feels clearer straight away.

A PHOTO TO TREASURE

This is a photo of me, aged four, in 1953. I am holding out a biscuit for Skippy, a dog who belonged to a lady who worked for the burlers and menders business with whom we shared our yard. The picture was published in The Catholic Universe newspaper.

Gloria Wilding, via email

Recipe of the week

HAM AND CAULIFLOWER CHEESE WITH MUSTARD

SERVES: **6 - 8** PREP: **10 mins** COOK: **2 hours**

2kg (4-5lb) gammon joint
2 tbsp Tracklements Robust Wholegrain Mustard
2 tbsp brown sugar
2 large cauliflowers, leaves cut off, broken into pieces
50g (2oz) butter
80g (3oz) plain flour
600ml (1pt) milk
Pepper to taste
250g (9oz) grated Cheddar cheese

1. Preheat the oven to 160C/140C Fan/Gas Mark 3.
2. Place the gammon, skin side up, into a pan and cover with cold water. Heat until it just starts to simmer, then remove from the heat and throw away the water.
3. Lay out the foil and place the ham skin side up in the middle and wrap the foil up to create a tent, which is tightly sealed but with room for air to circulate.
4. Bake for 1 hour then remove the foil and turn the oven up to 220C/200C Fan/Gas Mark 7.
5. Mix the mustard and brown sugar into a paste.
6. Cook the cauliflower in boiling water for 3-4 mins, then place in a roasting tray.
7. Next, make the cheese sauce: melt the butter in a saucepan, stir in the flour and slowly pour in the milk, whisking constantly to form a smooth sauce, then season to taste. Simmer for 5 mins, stirring, and add the cheese. Loosen with a little extra milk if needed. Pour the sauce over the cauliflower in the roasting tray and sprinkle with some extra cheese.
8. Cut the string and skin on the meat to leave a thin, even layer of fat. Score the fat into a diamond pattern.
9. Brush the mustard mixture all over the ham.
10. Place the ham, fat side up, in the middle of the cauliflower cheese and cook for a further 30 mins.

TRACKLEMENTS

29 SUNDAY

30 MONDAY

1 TUESDAY

2 WEDNESDAY

3 THURSDAY

4 FRIDAY

5 SATURDAY

On this week...

October 3rd 1952

PUT THE KETTLE ON!

News that tea rationing was to come to an end meant Britons could once again enjoy unlimited cuppas for the first time in 12 years. Minister of Food, Major Gwilym Lloyd-George, made the announcement during a speech in Newcastle, adding that the price of tea should not rise. Tea had first gone on wartime ration in July 1940. The ration was 2oz of tea for an adult, per week, which would allow a person about three cups of tea daily.

From July 1942, children under five received no tea ration, and people over 70 were granted an additional allowance from December 1944 onwards.

Although tea rationing came to an end in October 1952, the bad news for those who liked a bit of sweet in their tea was that sugar stayed on the ration for another five months, until February 1953.

Fun anagram!
Change pool into a sport

Answer: Polo

Money-saving tip

Don't let your old tech sit around the house gathering dust. Sites such as WeBuyBooks, Music Magpie, CeX and Ziffit will buy old books, mobiles, CDs and DVDs, etc. You'll be given an estimated price they'll pay you and it's usually free to post your items.

Mood boosters

An open chicken and salad sandwich for lunch will keep you going all afternoon. Having just one slice of bread per sandwich increases the protein-to-carbs ratio to keep your blood sugar steady after the meal so your body's cells will have a stable energy supply to keep you energised!

A PHOTO TO TREASURE

This picture shows me, aged two, having a picnic with my many dolls and toy animals. Larry the Lamb was a constant companion, as were Sooty and Rubberneck, my plastic fish. I also had several teddies. I loved them all and could never decide which was my favourite.

Linda Kettle, Portsmouth

Recipe of the week

GRAIN-FREE PECAN PIE

SERVES: **12** PREP: **30 mins** COOK: **40 mins**

For the pastry:
70g (2½ oz) chestnut flour
85g (3oz) The Groovy Food Company Organic Coconut Flour
Pinch of sea salt
140g (5oz) The Groovy Food Company Organic Virgin Coconut Oil
100g (4oz) pecan halves

For the filling:
110g (4oz) The Groovy Food Company Organic Virgin Coconut Oil
110g (4oz) The Groovy Food Company Organic Agave Nectar, light amber
200g (8oz) The Groovy Food Company Organic Coconut Sugar
3 large eggs, beaten

For the garnish:
Dairy-free cream/ice cream

1. Preheat the oven to 180C/160C Fan/Gas Mark 4. You will need a non-stick 9in loose bottom tart tin.
2. Place all the flours in a bowl with the salt and coconut oil and form into a ball. Place the ball in the base of the tin and smooth out and up the sides. Refrigerate the pastry case for 30 mins.
3. Roast the pecans in the oven for 10-12 mins, stirring a few times so they don't burn. Set aside and let them cool.
4. In a saucepan, melt the coconut oil, agave syrup and coconut sugar until smooth and soft. Remove the saucepan from the heat and leave to cool for 5-10 mins.
5. Add the beaten eggs to the mixture and stir.
6. Remove the pasty case from the fridge, pour in the melted mixture and decorate with the roasted pecan halves flat side down.
7. Place into oven for 45-50 mins. Check on the pie after 35 mins as you may want to add a sheet of foil over the pie to prevent the crust and nuts from burning.
8. The mixture will rise in the oven, but don't be alarmed – once out of the oven it will return to its natural shape.
9. Serve with cream or ice cream.

THE GROOVY FOOD COMPANY

6 SUNDAY

7 MONDAY

8 TUESDAY

9 WEDNESDAY

10 THURSDAY

11 FRIDAY

12 SATURDAY

On this week...

October 6th 1952

THE MOUSE THAT ROARED

Agatha Christie's play, The Mousetrap, had its world premier at the Theatre Royal Nottingham (later moving to the West End). The whodunnit ends with a clever twist, which the audience is traditionally asked not to reveal after leaving the theatre.

The production is a record breaker, clocking up more than 27,000 performances and having run continuously for 72 years (bar an enforced break during the pandemic).

Over the years more than 400 actors have played the eight character roles. Richard Attenborough was the original Detective Sergeant Trotter, and his wife, Sheila Sim, the first Mollie Ralston.

Mathew Prichard, Christie's grandson, was given the rights to the play for his birthday. The contract terms state that the identity of the perpetrator is to be kept secret – and no film adaptation can be produced until six months after the end of the West End production. With the play's ongoing popularity, this may never happen!

Fun anagram!
Change silent into something you must do at school

Answer: Listen

Money-saving tip

The Boots Advantage card is one of the most generous in terms of rewards, and seniors (aged 60 plus) get an added boost – receiving eight points per £1 spent, rather than the usual four. You also get access to special in-store events, which can offer free gifts and discounts, including on Boots opticians.

Mood boosters

As a child, a Sunday night bath was a ritual, but most of us have fallen out of the habit. A regular soak – three to four times a week – could lower your risk of heart attack and stroke and improve blood pressure, but it's also calming. Light a candle, add bubbles and play relaxing music to up the effects.

A PHOTO TO TREASURE

This is the last photo taken of my dad and the first one ever taken with all four of his grandchildren. As he'd been unable to attend my son Richard's wedding, we recreated the occasion in his care home, dressed in our finery with readings, cake and champagne.

Joy Harris, via email

Recipe of the week

MOROCCAN-STYLE VEGETABLE TAGINE

SERVES: **4** PREP: **10 mins** COOK: **30 mins**

1 tbsp Mr Organic Olive Oil
2 onions, chopped
½ tsp salt
2 carrots, chopped
1 sweet potato, peeled and chopped
1 small courgette, chopped
1 red bell pepper, chopped
Handful of cauliflower florets (optional)
5 garlic cloves, crushed or grated
2 tsp finely grated ginger
1 tbsp ras el hanout
1 tsp smoked paprika powder
1 tsp sweet paprika powder
1 tsp turmeric
½ tsp ground cumin
1 tbsp Mr Organic Light Agave Syrup
400ml (14fl oz) Mr Organic Tomato Passata
300ml (10fl oz) vegetable stock
1 tin Mr Organic Chickpeas, drained
Juice of 1 lemon
1 tbsp Mr Organic Balsamic Glaze
Dairy-free yogurt and fresh coriander or mint leaves, to serve

1. Heat the olive oil in a large skillet over a medium heat, then add the chopped onions and sprinkle with salt. Sauté for 2 mins, then add the carrots, sweet potato, courgette, bell pepper and cauliflower. Sauté for a further 15 mins, while stirring regularly.
2. Next, add your garlic, ginger and spices to the skillet and stir to evenly coat the veggies in the flavours. Add the agave syrup, then pour in the tomato passata and vegetable stock.
3. Cover and bring to a simmer. Cook for 10-15 mins or until the carrots and cauliflower are soft. Stir in the chickpeas and remove from the heat after another 5 mins.
4. Lastly, stir through the lemon juice and balsamic glaze, and serve alongside a dollop of dairy-free yogurt and fresh coriander or mint leaves.

MR ORGANIC

13 SUNDAY

14 MONDAY

15 TUESDAY

16 WEDNESDAY

17 THURSDAY

18 FRIDAY

19 SATURDAY

On this week...

October 19th 1952

AN ACT OF BRAVERY

John Bamford (15) became the youngest person to be awarded the George Cross after he rescued his two young brothers from their upstairs bedroom after a fire ripped through their house in Newthorpe, Notts.

After a fast-spreading fire broke out in their home, John and his father attempted to rescue his five siblings. After helping three of the children and their mother on to the flat roof, John and his father headed to the back bedroom where they could hear the two remaining children, aged 4 and 6, shouting.

The father draped a blanket around himself and attempted to reach the children but it caught fire and he was driven back. John told his father to go to the back of the house while he got down on his hands and knees and crawled through the flames into the bedroom.

His shirt was burned but, nevertheless, he snatched the two young boys from the bed and managed to get them to a window. John was praised for displaying courage of the highest order, despite serious burns.

Fun anagram!
Change runes into a job

Answer: Nurse

Money-saving tip

Challenge yourself to having a regular 'make money day' where you find things from your home and list them online on sites such as Vinted, Gumtree and Facebook Marketplace, or even on your WhatsApp groups. Even unlikely things – such as used make-up – can have a market, especially if it's from a discontinued or pricey line.

Mood boosters

Get your wool and knitting needles out! Knitting has been found to have a meditative effect on the brain and the repetitive, soothing motion of the needles helps release the happy hormone serotonin. You might find yourself zoning out and having a mindful moment without even trying!

A PHOTO TO TREASURE

This photo is of my cousin Iris who was in the army during the Second World War. I believe she worked in the War Office, but as she had signed the Official Secrets Act she would never say. She was broken hearted when her romance with an American officer ended when he returned home after the war.

Valerie Reilly, via email

Recipe of the week

PUMPKIN SPICE MUFFINS

MAKES: **12** PREP: **10 mins** COOK: **30 mins**

215g (8oz) pumpkin puree (this comes in a can and is available in supermarkets)
2 eggs
125ml/g (4fl oz) sunflower or vegetable oil
75ml/g (3fl oz) water
300g (11oz) caster sugar
225g (8oz) self raising flour
1 tsp bicarbonate of soda
3 tsp mixed spice
Pumpkin seeds

1. Preheat the oven to 180C/160C Fan/Gas Mark 4.
2. In a large mixing bowl, whisk together the pumpkin puree, eggs, oil and water, then add in the sugar, flour, bicarbonate of soda and mixed spices and whisk until a smooth batter is formed.
3. Divide the batter evenly between the muffin cases, top with a sprinkling of pumpkin seeds and bake for 25-30 mins until risen, golden and springy to the touch.
4. Allow to cool before serving.

EASY PEASY BAKING CAMPAIGN

20 SUNDAY

21 MONDAY

22 TUESDAY

23 WEDNESDAY

24 THURSDAY

25 FRIDAY

26 SATURDAY

On this week...

October 21st 1964

SINGING SNUBBED

The film version of My Fair Lady, directed by George Cukor and starring Audrey Hepburn, premiered in New York. Audrey played Eliza Doolittle, and replaced Julie Andrews who played the character in the stage musical. Audrey, who did not have the same vocal talent as Andrews, was informed she would have to be dubbed. She reportedly walked off set, but returned the next day and, in a typically graceful Hepburn gesture, apologised for her "wicked behaviour".

Audrey later admitted she would never have accepted the role of Eliza Doolittle if she had known that producer Jack L. Warner intended to have nearly all of her singing dubbed. After making this movie, she resolved not to appear in another movie musical unless she could do the singing on her own. The film was both a critical and commercial success, becoming the highest-grossing film of 1964 and winning eight Academy Awards. In 1998, the American Film Institute named it the 91st greatest American film of all time.

Fun anagram!
Change taxes into an American state

Answer: Texas

Money-saving tip

Save money on your car insurance by being organised and setting a reminder before it's time to renew – the average motorist will pay 17 per cent less for a new quote with more than a week to go on their policy than if they renew on the last day.

Mood boosters

Go back through your old photo albums, diaries, letters or memories and try to find a truly happy occasion when you were left helpless with a fit of the giggles. Try to reconnect with how you felt then – laugh now as you did then.

A PHOTO TO TREASURE

Thanks to a street photographer, I have this precious memory of me with my mother in 1946. We had few treats as money was short, but in the school holidays Mother and I donned our best clothes, had lunch in a Lyons corner house then went window shopping in Oxford Street.

Sylvia Monk, via email

Recipe of the week

VEGAN CINNAMON TEAR AND SHARE LOAF

MAKES: **1 loaf** PREP: **35 mins** COOK: **25 mins**

60g (2oz) vegan spread
200ml (7fl oz) water
1 tsp fast action yeast
150g (5oz) wholemeal flour
150g (5oz) plain flour
90g (3oz) brown sugar (split into 30g (1oz) and 60g (2oz)
1 tsp ground cinnamon
2 tbsp ground flaxseeds
200g (8oz) icing sugar

1. Put 30g (1oz) of the vegan spread in a jug and melt in the microwave. Top up with 165ml (6fl oz) of warm water from the tap and stir in the yeast.
2. Combine the flours and 30g (1oz) of brown sugar in a large mixing bowl and pour in the yeast/water/spread mixture. Bring together to form a dough with your hands.
3. Tip the dough out onto a lightly floured surface and knead for 5 mins. Return to the mixing bowl, cover with a tea towel and leave to prove for 20 mins. After 10 mins, preheat the oven to 200C/185C Fan/Gas Mark 6 and grease a loaf tin with vegan spread.
4. After the dough has proved for 20 mins, tip it onto a lightly floured surface and roll it out into a 30cm x 30cm square. Spread the remaining 30g (1oz) of vegan spread evenly over the dough with the back of a spoon, then sprinkle the cinnamon, flaxseeds and remaining 60g (2oz) brown sugar. Roll the dough into a sausage shape.
5. Divide the dough into 6 equal pieces (5cm each) and place into the greased loaf tin, spirals facing up. Bake for 20-25 mins, turning the tin in the oven after 10 mins.
6. Rinse the jug, measure 35ml of cold tap water and mix in the icing sugar to make a glaze. Once the loaf has finished baking, allow it to cool slightly before removing from the tin and drizzling with the glaze. Tear and enjoy!

@BARITHEDIETITIAN FOR NOURISHING THE NATION

27 SUNDAY

28 MONDAY

29 TUESDAY

30 WEDNESDAY

31 THURSDAY

1 FRIDAY

2 SATURDAY

On this week...

October 27th 1952

CROCODILE ROCKER

Elton John's Crocodile Rock was released in the UK. Written by Elton and his long-term collaborator Bernie Taupin, the track was recorded earlier in the summer at the Chateau d'Herouville in France for the Don't Shoot Me I'm Only The Piano Player album. The song, written as a fun, nostalgic pastiche of the rock 'n' roll hits the songwriting partners had grown up with, went on to become one of Elton's biggest and best-remembered hits. It became his first US No.1 and secured success for the star Stateside.

Elton has played the song live numerous times over the years but, in 2021, he revealed that Crocodile Rock was written as a "kind of a joke" and that he doesn't enjoy playing it.

He went on to say that he'd continued to sing it at concerts because fans enjoy it, but vowed that he would never sing it again once the Goodbye Yellow Brick Road Tour came to an end in 2023.

Fun anagram!
Change there into a number

Answer: Three

Money-saving tip

Make money by selling unwanted clothes on eBay. Selling lots of cheaper items as a bundle is usually more economical, but always sell expensive branded goods separately for the best price. Keep an eye out for eBay promotions – especially weekend deals where seller fees are discounted or capped.

Mood boosters

A cuppa can transform your mood – chose chamomile, bergamot or lemon balm to calm before bed; choose blue vervain, valerian and hops to help you sleep. A lavender infusion isn't just soporific, it can comfort by reminding you of treasured childhood wind-down routines.

A PHOTO TO TREASURE

This is one of the few photos I have of my granny, Rosie. I am named after her as Rose is my middle name. Sadly, she died before I was born, but I feel as if I know her because of all the wonderful stories my family tell about her.

Sharon Haston, via email

Recipe of the week

GHOST MERINGUES

SERVES: **8** PREP: **10 mins** COOK: **2 hours**

The water from a can of Mr Organic Chickpeas
1 tsp of cream of tartar
150g (5oz) of icing sugar
1-2tsp of Mr Organic Chocolate Spread

1. Preheat your oven to 130C/120C Fan/Gas Mark 1/2.
2. Place the chickpea water into a large mixing bowl. Add the cream of tartar and whisk it with an electric whisk for 5-7 mins until you get stiff peaks.
3. Slowly add in the icing sugar whilst continuing to whisk. You should end up with a glossy, fluffy mixture.
4. Transfer the mixture to a piping bag with a round nozzle and pipe your ghost shapes onto a lined baking tray.
5. Transfer to the oven and bake for 2 hours. Leave the ghosts in the oven to cool down entirely, then remove.
6. Melt 1-2 tsp of Mr Organic chocolate spread and use a toothpick to carefully add eyes and mouths onto your ghosts.

MR ORGANIC

3 SUNDAY

4 MONDAY

5 TUESDAY

6 WEDNESDAY

7 THURSDAY

8 FRIDAY

9 SATURDAY

On this week...

November 7th 1980

END OF A HOLLYWOOD ERA

Hollywood lost one of its best-loved actors on this day in 1980 when American movie star Steve McQueen – largely known for his portrayal of macho loners in legendary epics The Great Escape (1963) and Bullitt (1968) – died of cancer at the age of just 50. The King of Cool dominated the big screen in the Sixties and Seventies, making his debut in The Blob (1955), aged just 28. But it was as the motorbike-racing, German prison camp-escaping airman Virgil Hilts that McQueen is perhaps best remembered.

Starring alongside James Garner and Richard Attenborough, Hilts' iconic motorbike jump is one of the film world's most memorable scenes. And while McQueen was often cited as having made the jump himself, it later transpired that it was his friend and body double, Bud Ekins, who performed the stunt.

Fun anagram!

Change canoe into a word used in geography

Answer: Ocean

Money-saving tip

Turn your oven off ten minutes before your food is ready – it will keep on cooking but you'll save on energy costs. Maximise oven time by batch cooking, and cook in glass or ceramic ovenware that retains heat better than metal.

Mood boosters

Need a quick surge of energy? Dark chocolate is your friend. Epicatechin, a plant chemical found in dark chocolate, can give your body a boost by widening your blood vessels. This lets more oxygen get to your muscles so everyday tasks seem easier.

A PHOTO TO TREASURE

This photo was taken in 1983, the first time my husband Bill and I had been abroad. We stayed at the Sol Pelicanos hotel, which featured in the television series, Benidorm. I was often mistaken for a Spanish lady as I have dark brown hair and used to wear a frilly red blouse.

Patricia Mason, via email

Recipe of the week

STICKY TOFFEE COOKIES

MAKES: **6 large cookies** PREP: **10 mins** COOK: **20 mins**

115g (4oz) unsalted butter, softened
150g (5oz) light brown sugar
1 egg
185g (7oz) wholemeal flour
50g (2oz) instant porridge (similar to Ready Brek)
½ tsp bicarbonate of soda
1 tsp flaky sea salt
100g (4oz) dates, chopped and soaked in 2 tbsp boiling water
50g (2oz) pecans, roughly chopped
200g (8oz) dark chocolate (you can use chips or bars cut into chunks)

1. Cream together the butter and light brown sugar, add the egg followed by the flour, oats, bicarbonate of soda and salt. Mix until large clumps start to appear.
2. Mash the soaked dates roughly with a fork and then add to the dough along with the pecans and chopped dark chocolate, reserving a few chunks to place on top of your cookies.
3. Bring the mixture together with your hands until a dough is formed, then divide evenly into 6 portions. Roll each portion into a ball, flatten lightly and place 2 chunks of chocolate into the top of each one.
4. Preheat your oven to 200C/180C Fan/Gas Mark 4 or, if using an air fryer, 180C and cook on a circle of parchment paper for 15-20 mins depending on how well done you like your cookies.

NOURISHING THE NATION

10 SUNDAY

11 MONDAY

12 TUESDAY

13 WEDNESDAY

14 THURSDAY

15 FRIDAY

16 SATURDAY

On this week...

November 14th 1952

NO.1 CHART TOPPER

The UK's first singles chart – Record Hit Parade – was published, and Here in My Heart by Al Martino was the first No.1. The chart was planned as a Top 12, but there were 15 records on it due to ties at Nos. 6, 7 and 11. Other hits included Jo Stafford at No.2 with You Belong to Me and Nat King Cole in third place with Somewhere Along the Way.

The chart was the brainchild of Percy Dickins who co-founded NME magazine with journalist Ray Sonin. Dickins, who was responsible for advertising sales, predicted that a weekly record chart would attract record company ads to the paper.

Rather than compiling actual sales figures, Dickens called stores asking for weekly best sellers. He awarded 20 points to the top seller at each store, 19 points to the second, and so on, then tallied up the totals to compile a singles chart. A version of his method became the standard way of compiling charts for many years.

Fun anagram!

Change tuna into a member of the family

Answer: Aunt

Money-saving tip

Electric blankets are an affordable purchase that will save you money in the long run. Set it on a timer an hour before bedtime and your bed will be toasty and you'll be able to turn your central heating off earlier, saving you money.

Mood boosters

Mushrooms are the only plant source of natural vitamin D, and foods that contain vitamin D boost serotonin in the brain making you feel happier. When it's dark outdoors, up your intake of vitamin D with a supplement but also add mushrooms to your risottos, omelettes and soups.

A PHOTO TO TREASURE

This is me (dressed in white) when I was a children's entertainer at Filey in 1978. Aged 19, I loved all the activities, especially the magic shows. Despite the long hours and the draughty caravan, it was an enriching experience and helped me to get an Equity card.

Heather Moulson, via email

Recipe of the week

CHILLI PARTY POTATO SKINS

SERVES: **3-4** PREP: **5 mins** COOK: **40 mins**

4 medium sweet potatoes
2 tbsp Mr Organic Rapeseed Oil
1 large red onion, finely diced
3 cloves garlic, crushed
½ tsp salt
1 fresh red chilli, finely diced
½ green pepper, finely diced
1 sweet red pepper, finely diced
1 tin Mr Organic Mixed Beans, drained
1 tin Mr Organic Black Beans, drained
1 tin Mr Organic Chopped Tomatoes
1 tablespoon smoked paprika
300ml (10fl oz) vegetable stock
150g (5oz) tinned sweetcorn, drained
3-4 tbsp pineapple chunks
3-4 slices vegan cheese
Coconut yoghurt or guacamole and fresh coriander

1. Slice the potatoes in half and pierce with a knife.
2. Preheat your oven to 200°C/18C Fan/Gas Mark 6, then place the potato halves on a lined baking tray. Drizzle with half of the oil, then roast for 20 to 30 mins.
3. To prepare the chilli, heat the rest of the oil in a pan, then cook the red onion for 4-5 mins. Add the garlic, salt, chilli and green and red peppers, beans, tomatoes and smoked paprika for another min.
4. Pour the stock and bring to a simmer. Cook for 30-35 mins. Stir in the sweetcorn and remove from the heat. Blend half of your chilli mixture and stir it with the rest.
5. Remove the potatoes from the oven and use a spoon to scoop out about 1-2cm of the flesh. Transfer to the fridge or freezer to use in a future recipe.
6. Fill your sweet potato skins with the chilli, top with pineapple chunks and a sprinkle of vegan cheese.
7. Place the potato skins under the grill for 2 to 3 mins.
8 Serve your sweet potato skins with a drizzle of coconut yoghurt or guacamole and fresh coriander on top.

MR ORGANIC

17 SUNDAY

18 MONDAY

19 TUESDAY

20 WEDNESDAY

21 THURSDAY

22 FRIDAY

23 SATURDAY

On this week...

November 20th 1982

SAMURAI SOLDIERS

Richard Chamberlain wielded his Samurai sword in the mini-series Shogun. Based on the James Clavell novel of the same name, it told the tale of the adventures of Englishman John Blackthorne who, after being shipwrecked, becomes trapped in 17th century Japan. He becomes embroiled in a battle between two feudal warlords who both want to claim the title Shogun. The success of the mini-series increased awareness and interest in Japanese culture and was credited with propelling the paperback edition of Clavell's novel to become a 2.1 million copy bestseller.

Fun anagram!
Change **harks** into a dangerous animal

Answer: Shark

Money-saving tip

Keep your home warm by fitting draught excluders around windows and doors, letterbox brushes, chimney balloons and keyhole coverings to help keep cold air out. Hang curtains so that the thick material will prevent heat being lost through the window (keep them open in the day so any sun can help warm the room).

Mood boosters

Reclaim Sunday afternoons as your time to get crafty – absorbing pastimes are key to finding your flow, which leads to happiness. Create your own woven paper hearts for an instant mood-booster, learn to make jewellery or to weave. See abeautifulmess.com for more ideas.

A PHOTO TO TREASURE

This cool-looking Teddy Boy is my dad, Ray Palmer, lounging by the motorbike which was his pride and joy. He would repeatedly drive up and down the street where my mum lived, determined to catch her eye. I'm pleased to say he succeeded and after they were married she rode pillion.

Sharon Palmer, via email

Recipe of the week

PUMPKIN POLENTA WITH BALSAMIC BEETS

SERVES: **3-4** PREP: **30 mins** COOK: **30 mins**

300g (10½oz) beetroot, peeled and chopped
1 tbsp olive oil
2 tbsp Mr Organic Balsamic Vinegar
½ tsp salt
100g (3½oz) Mr Organic Black Beans
1 tbsp dairy-free spread
1 small yellow onion
¼ tsp sea salt flakes
2 cloves garlic, crushed
750ml (25fl oz) veg stock
250g (9oz) polenta
150g (5oz) pumpkin puree
2 tbsp nutritional yeast
1 tsp white miso paste
100-150ml (3-5fl oz) almond milk
Salt & black pepper to taste

1. Preheat oven to 200C/180C Fan/Gas Mark 6.
2. Toss the beetroot into a mixing bowl to evenly coat with the olive oil and balsamic vinegar. Transfer onto a lined baking tray or oven dish, sprinkle with salt and roast in the middle of the oven for 30-35 mins. Stir the black beans into the roasted balsamic beets and set aside.
3. In the meantime, melt the dairy-free spread in a large saucepan over a medium heat, then add in the onion, salt and garlic and sauté until translucent. Pour in the vegetable stock and then slowly stir in the polenta. It's best to use a whisk to avoid any lumps. Reduce the heat to low and allow for the polenta to cook for a few mins until the mixture thickens. Stir continuously.
4. Add in the pumpkin puree, nutritional yeast and white miso paste and, once heated through, remove from the heat and stir in the almond milk until you get to your desired creamy texture. Season to taste and garnish with balsamic roasted beets and black beans.

MR ORGANIC

24 SUNDAY

25 MONDAY

26 TUESDAY

27 WEDNESDAY

28 THURSDAY

29 FRIDAY

30 SATURDAY

On this week...

November 26th 1942

A CLASSIC IS BORN

The film Casablanca, directed by Michael Curtiz and starring Humphrey Bogart and Ingrid Bergman, premiered at the Hollywood Theatre in New York. Casablanca was nominated for eight Academy Awards and won three, including Best Picture.

It was also a box office hit, receiving unexpected publicity from the Allied landing in the real city of Casablanca in November 1942, and from the summit conference held there by US President Franklin D. Roosevelt and British Prime Minister Winston Churchill two months later.

Acclaimed for its snappy dialogue, Casablanca is the source of several classic movie quotes, perhaps most notably a line Rick affectionately repeats to Ilsa: "Here's looking at you, kid."

Fun anagram!
Change **prides** into an insect

Answer: Spider

Money-saving tip

Consider getting a smart thermostat, which controls your central heating and can be controlled remotely via an app on your phone or tablet. It will help you understand how much energy you are using and give real time energy consumption data, which can help you save money.

Mood boosters

Create your own sanctuary in your home as the spot you go to centre yourself. It could be as simple as positioning a comfy chair towards a window with a view of the outdoors and planting a small window box on the ledge, or having a fruit bowl or flowers in sight. Add a blanket for extra cosiness.

A PHOTO TO TREASURE

My dad, Percy, is standing on the right in this family photo taken in the yard of their two-up two-down terraced house. 'Mod cons' consisted of cold water from a pump and an outside loo. His ten siblings shared one big bed with the girls at one end and the boys at the other.

Barbara Girling, Suffolk

Recipe of the week

GINGERBREAD TRAYBAKE CAKE

MAKES: **1** PREP: **15 mins** COOK: **30mins**

200g (7oz) unsalted butter + 40g (1½oz) for icing
150g (5oz) light brown sugar
4 tbsp black treacle
2 eggs
300g (11oz) self raising flour
1 tbsp ground ginger
150ml (5fl oz) milk
75g (3oz) cream cheese
200g (7oz) icing sugar
Crushed gingerbread men, to decorate

1. Preheat the oven to 180C/160 Fan/Gas Mark 4.
2. In a mixing bowl, cream together the butter and sugar until light and fluffy. Add in the treacle and eggs, followed by the flour, ginger and milk, mixing after each addition until a thick, smooth batter is formed.
3. Pour the batter into a greased, lined tin and bake for 25-30 mins until risen and springy to the touch. Allow to cool completely.
4. Make the icing by combining the 40g of butter, cream cheese and icing sugar until no lumps remain. Using a palette knife or the back of a spoon, spread evenly on top of the ginger sponge and sprinkle with crushed gingerbread men.

EASY PEASY BAKING CAMPAIGN

1 SUNDAY

2 MONDAY

3 TUESDAY

4 WEDNESDAY

5 THURSDAY

6 FRIDAY

7 SATURDAY

On this week...

December 5th 1952

LONDON'S GREAT SMOG

A killer fog descended on London, bringing the capital to a standstill, with people only able to see a few hundred yards ahead of them. The Great Smog (as it became known) was a severe air pollution event that affected London.

A period of cold weather, combined with an anticyclone and windless conditions, collected airborne pollutants – mostly arising from the use of coal – to form a thick layer of smog, which lasted from Friday 5 December to Tuesday 9 December 1952.

The smog caused major disruption by reducing visibility and penetrating indoor areas. Government medical reports in the weeks following the event estimated that up to 4,000 people had died as a direct result of the smog and 100,000 more were made ill by its effects on the respiratory tract.

More recent research suggests that the total number of fatalities may have been considerably greater, with estimates of between 10,000 and 12,000 deaths.

Fun anagram!
Change act into an animal

Answer: Cat

Money-saving tip

Putting silver foil behind a radiator will help reflect heat back into the room, helping to save money by preserving heat. Wrap foil around cardboard to fit behind radiators or use specialist radiator foil. (The only time it won't work is if you have cavity wall insulation.)

Mood boosters

Ward off colds with New Zealand Manuka honey, which has proven anti-microbial properties. Buy the highest level of MGO Manuka honey you can afford, and eat it straight or add it to food. We like to add a teaspoon to hot water and lemon for a traditional remedy.

A PHOTO TO TREASURE

These are our grandchildren, Theia and Albie, taken at Theia's first school nativity play. Each year they surprise us with how much they are learning and thriving. To us, they are simply little cherubs – although our daughter tells us a different story sometimes!

Jackie Perrins, via email

Recipe of the week

CAULIFLOWER AND ROASTED GARLIC SOUP

SERVES: **4** PREP: **5 mins** COOK: **1 hour**

1 whole garlic bulb
2 tbsp of olive oil, plus extra for garnish
1 leek, chopped
1 stick of celery, chopped
1 whole cauliflower, roughly broken
1 pint of vegetable stock
100g (4oz) Stilton
4 slices of sourdough or any bread you have (the ends work well)
Salt and pepper

1. Cut the top off of the garlic bulb, put in some tinfoil, drizzle with oil and scrunch up the tinfoil to make a parcel and pop in the oven for 30 mins at 180C/160C Fan/Gas Mark 4.
2. Meanwhile, in a deep pan, heat the olive oil and cook the leek and celery until soft.
3. Add the broken up cauliflower to the pan, pour in the vegetable stock, pop the lid on, bring to the boil then simmer for roughly 30 mins.
4. Add the Stilton to the slices of bread and pop under a high grill until it's melted and golden brown.
5. Once all the veg is soft and cooked through, squeeze out all the garlic cloves into the soup and blitz with a handheld mixer or blender until you have a smooth soup. Season to taste.
6. Top with the Stilton croutons, drizzle olive oil around, and add extra Stilton if you want.

LONG CLAWSON DAIRY

8 SUNDAY

9 MONDAY

10 TUESDAY

11 WEDNESDAY

12 THURSDAY

13 FRIDAY

14 SATURDAY

On this week...

December 10th 1962

DESERT DEBUT

David Lean's dazzling epic, Lawrence of Arabia, had its world premiere in Leicester Square. Queen Elizabeth II and the Duke of Edinburgh were present, but the film almost wasn't! Just 48 hours earlier one of only two original prints of the film got scratched and the other was at London airport waiting to be despatched to New York. Film editor Anne V. Coates, who had worked on the film for the previous four months, was sent to retrieve the print and save the premiere.

As the royal couple were introduced to the cast and crew, the Duke of Edinburgh turned to Lean and asked, "Good flick?". "I hope so," Lean replied, bristling slightly. He needn't have worried; as soon as the audience saw the scale and majesty of the images on screen, they were transported by the masterpiece.

Peter O'Toole's spectacular performance earned him an Oscar nomination and a quip from Noël Coward saying, "Had O'Toole been any prettier, the film would have had to be renamed Florence of Arabia."

Fun anagram!
Change ones into a part of the body

Answer: Nose

Money-saving tip

If you only want to heat one room in your house, it's not necessarily cheaper to run an electric heater (it will depend on how efficient the model is plus ceiling height and the insulation of your room). Central heating is still cheaper to run – just use thermostats to only heat the rooms you need.

Mood boosters

Crank up the volume and get the carols blasting out! Listening to loud music helps to improve energy levels and could help to lift your mood. Upbeat tunes trigger positive memories too – how about a little Rocking Around the Christmas Tree?

A PHOTO TO TREASURE

Thanks to her popularity as the lollipop lady at Sedgefield Primary School, my late wife Barbara was always a welcome choice to assist at various community events. Here she is as the reindeer leading the snowman parade in December 2013.
John Nicholls, via email

Recipe of the week

CHOCOLATE ORANGE SHORTBREAD SANDWICHES

MAKES: **9** PREP: **25 mins** COOK: **12 mins**

200g (8oz) unsalted butter (room temperature)
100g (4oz) caster sugar
250g (10oz) plain flour
50g (2oz) cornflour
1 orange
150g (5oz) dark or milk chocolate
Icing sugar for dusting

1. Preheat the oven to 200C/180C Fan/Gas Mark 6.
2. In a bowl, cream together the butter and sugar with a spoon.
3. Add in the flour, cornflour and the zest of the orange and mix by rubbing between your fingertips until a crumb consistency is achieved, then bring together into a dough.
4. Turn the dough out, flatten into a rectangle shape, wrap in cling film and place in the freezer for 15 mins.
5. While the dough is chilling, melt the chocolate in the microwave in 30 second blasts, stirring at intervals. When it is completely melted, combine with 75g (3oz) of fresh juice squeezed from the orange. Set to one side.
6. Roll the chilled dough out to a 5mm (3/16in) thickness on a lightly floured surface. Cut out rounds and place them on the lined baking tray.
7. Bring the offcuts together, roll out and continue to cut rounds until all of the dough has been used up.
8. Cut stars out of the centres of half of the rounds, placing them on the tray in between the rounds.
9. Bake for 12 mins, then allow to cool.
10. Use a spoon to spread the chocolate filling on the base biscuits, then sandwich with the star-centre top biscuits. Dust with icing sugar and serve.

EASY PEASY BAKING CAMPAIGN

15 SUNDAY

16 MONDAY

17 TUESDAY

18 WEDNESDAY

19 THURSDAY

20 FRIDAY

21 SATURDAY

On this week...

December 15th 1982

A NEW FRONTIER

The gates between Gibraltar and Spain were opened for the first time in 13 years, allowing pedestrians to travel between the island and the mainland. The new Spanish government cited 'humanitarian' reasons for opening the frontier. A Spanish police official in plain clothes unceremoniously unlocked the gates for both sides.

A crowd of several thousand sightseers in festive spirit gathered to celebrate the momentous occasion as students performed an impromptu live music session. There were several hundred Gibraltarian well-wishers on the other side.

Despite the good will gesture by the Spanish authorities, the frontier opened under tight restrictions, which included a ban on any British or foreign tourists crossing. Only Spanish citizens or inhabitants of Gibraltar were allowed across.

Fun anagram!

Change **cosmic** into things you read

Answer: Comics

Money-saving tip

Lighting accounts for around 15 per cent of home electricity use, so always turn lights off when you leave a room (it's a myth that turning them on and off uses more electricity than if you just leave lights on).

Mood boosters

Lighting candles is an instant way to make your room cosy and help you feel comfy. The Danish (who are experts at hygge – all things cosy) have a word for spoilsport, which is lyselukker – it means "the one who put out the candle!" Choose a natural, organic one for calming vibes.

A PHOTO TO TREASURE

The top photo is of me and my sister Angela taken with a very miserable Father Christmas 50 years ago. The bottom picture shows the replica we made with my husband being a good sport and playing Santa. It made the family laugh!

Janet South, via email

Recipe of the week

POTATO STUFFING CHRISTMAS WREATH

SERVES: **6** PREP:**15 mins** COOK: **40 mins**

1 tbsp olive oil
400g (14oz) white potatoes
Large pinch of salt & pepper
3 sprigs each of fresh rosemary and thyme
1 red onion
5 cloves garlic
1 tsp each of dried rosemary, thyme and sage
100g (4oz) mixed chopped nuts
1 tbsp tomato puree
80ml (3fl oz) water
2 tbsp cranberry sauce

1. Preheat the oven to 200C/180C Fan/Gas Mark 6, drizzle olive oil onto a baking tray and pop in the oven to warm up.
2. Quarter the potatoes and add to the tray with the hot oil, sprinkle with salt and a few sprigs of fresh rosemary, then bake for around 25 mins.
3. Prepare the filling by dicing the onion and fry it in a pan with a drizzle of olive oil for around 4 mins.
4. Finely chop the garlic cloves and add to the pan with the onion. Toss in the dried rosemary, sage and thyme, and mixed chopped nuts and fry for around 6-7 mins.
5. Add the tomato puree with a dash of water and mix until combined. Set aside.
6. Once the potatoes have roasted, add to the pan then roughly mash together before adding to a greased baking sheet. Mould to the shape of a wreath and bake for a further 20 mins.
7. Take out once crispy, then drizzle a little cranberry sauce over the top and add a few sprigs of thyme.

SEASONAL SPUDS

22 SUNDAY

23 MONDAY

24 TUESDAY

25 WEDNESDAY

26 THURSDAY

27 FRIDAY

28 SATURDAY

On this week...

December 25th 1952

NEW MONARCH'S FESTIVE MESSAGE

Millions of listeners tuned in to hear Queen Elizabeth II's first Christmas broadcast. In a tradition begun by her grandfather King George V, the new Queen made her BBC radio address from the study at her home in Sandringham, Norfolk.

The Queen began: "Each Christmas, at this time, my beloved father broadcast a message to his people in all parts of the world. Today I am doing this to you, who are now my people.

"As he used to do, I am speaking to you from my own home, where I am spending Christmas with my family."

She went on to give a special mention to the armed forces serving abroad and thanked her subjects for their loyalty and affection, making a pledge to continue the work of her father and grandfather to unite the nations of the Commonwealth and the Empire.

She ended with: "Wherever you are... I give you my affectionate greetings, with every good wish for Christmas and the New Year."

Fun anagram!
Change pains into a country

Answer: Spain

Money-saving tip

You could save over £100 a year by turning your heating down by 1°C from the average temperature of 20°C – but don't allow your home to get too chilly as if left cold for too long, damp and mould can form, which costs more to fix.

Mood boosters

If you suffer with low mood or anxiety, you may find some relief by increasing the amount of tryptophan-rich foods in your diet – this is used by the brain to produce the 'happy hormone' serotonin. Chicken, turkey, eggs, salmon, tuna, beans, lentils, dark green leafy vegetables, nuts and seeds are good sources, as is chocolate!

A PHOTO TO TREASURE

This photo was taken in 2005 when I had my three sons, my grandsons and my mother for Christmas dinner, cooked by my wonderful husband. That's me on the right in the pink cardigan. My grandsons have all grown into fine young men now.

Janet Dandy, vie email

Recipe of the week

BAILEYS PROFITEROLE STACK

MAKES: **36 profiteroles** PREP: **10 mins** COOK: **25 mins**

100g (4oz) butter, cut into 1cm cubes
250ml (2fl oz) water
140g (5oz) plain flour
4 eggs
600ml (20fl oz) double cream
200ml (7fl oz) Baileys, split into two batches of 100ml
200g (7oz) dark chocolate

1. Preheat the oven to 200C/180C Fan/Gas Mark 6.
2. Put the butter and water in a saucepan and heat until it comes to a boil. Turn off the heat and add in the flour, beating until a soft dough is formed.
3. Turn the heat back up to medium and cook out the flour for 3-4 mins, stirring constantly, before transferring to a large mixing bowl and leaving to cool.
4. Using an electric hand whisk, add the eggs one by one, until a smooth glossy paste is formed. Transfer the paste into a piping bag and cut a 1.5cm opening.
5. Pipe 18 small mounds onto each tray and bake for 20 mins until risen and golden brown. Leave to cool.
6. To make the cream filling, pour the cream and 100ml of Baileys into a mixing bowl and whisk until thick.
7. Once cool, cut each profiterole in half and spoon the cream into each one, being careful not to overfill.
8. Heat the other 100ml of Baileys in a saucepan until simmering, then remove from the heat and add in the dark chocolate, stirring continuously until a ganache.
9. Stack the profiteroles in a pyramid style on a serving plate, spooning the chocolate over each layer. Drizzle any remaining ganache over the completed stack.

EASY PEASY BAKING CAMPAIGN

29 SUNDAY

30 MONDAY

31 TUESDAY

1 WEDNESDAY

2 THURSDAY

3 FRIDAY

4 SATURDAY

On this week...

January 3rd 1963

SNOW STOPS PLAY

One of the coldest winters on record, 'The Big Freeze of 1963' caused widespread disruption. On December 29 and 30, 1962, a blizzard swept across South West England and Wales with snow drifting to more than 20ft deep in places, blocking roads and railways and bringing down power lines.

Continued near-freezing temperatures meant the snow cover lasted more than two months in some areas. In early January 1963, the upper reaches of the Thames froze over and the sea froze up to a mile offshore.

Sport was heavily disrupted. Football matches in the English and Scottish leagues were cancelled and some matches in the FA Cup ties were rescheduled ten or more times.

A special board, known as the Pools Panel, had to be set up to provide the football pools results. Five ex-footballers were tasked with adjudicating postponed matches by predicting what the score would have been had the match gone ahead.

Fun anagram!

Change the word fried into something you don't want to be at work

Answer: Fired

Money-saving tip

Carefully consider which cooking method you actually need to use. Using more efficient appliances could typically save households £287 a year. Electric cookers cost 87p per day to run, gas cookers 33p, slow cookers 16p, air fryers 14p and microwaves 8p.

Mood boosters

A lack of sleep can really affect your mood. Try a self-heating, night-time eye mask – they combine self-heating technology with calming lavender, chamomile and rose aromas to soothe tension and relax the muscles around the eyes to ease stress. Sweet dreams!

A PHOTO TO TREASURE

I love this photo of starlings in my snowy garden. They liked splashing around in the bird bath and looked puzzled to find the water turned to ice. They also liked to nest in the roof space above my home office and I grew used to their thumps and squawks overhead.

Catherine Reeve, via email

Recipe of the week

PARSNIP AND CHESTNUT RISOTTO

SERVES: **4** PREP: **5 mins** COOK: **25 mins**

2 tbsp olive oil
½ white onion, finely chopped
1 stick of celery, finely chopped
2 garlic cloves, crushed
350g (12oz) Arborio rice
1.5 litre (51fl oz) vegetable stock (use as needed)
250g (9oz) leftover roasted parsnips, cubed
1 handful of leftover cooked chestnuts, finely chopped
1 knob of salted butter
Freshly milled black pepper and salt to taste
100g (4oz) cooked leftover stuffing
4 sage leaves, finely chopped
20g (1oz) Parmesan, grated

1. Heat 1 tbsp of olive oil over a medium heat in a large pan with a lid and cook the white onion and celery for 1-2 mins. Add the garlic and cook for a further min. Add in the rice and stir. Bring to a boil.
2. Slowly incorporate the vegetable stock, stirring well at a simmer. Cook for a total of 15 mins until the rice is al dente.
3. Stir in cooked parsnips and chestnuts and season with a knob of butter, salt and pepper. Cover again and cook for a further 5 mins.
4. Add 1 tbsp of olive oil to a small pan and fry off the sage leaves and cooked stuffing until a crumb-like consistency and golden brown.
5. Serve the risotto with generous helpings of stuffing and sage mix and a sprinkle of grated parmesan.

SAM NIXON WITH ASDA

2024 year-to-view calendar

JANUARY						
M	1	8	15	22	29	
Tu	2	9	16	23	30	
W	3	10	17	24	31	
Th	4	11	18	25		
F	5	12	19	26		
Sa	6	13	20	27		
Su	7	14	21	28		

FEBRUARY						
M		5	12	19	26	
Tu		6	13	20	27	
W		7	14	21	28	
Th	1	8	15	22	29	
F	2	9	16	23		
Sa	3	10	17	24		
Su	4	11	18	25		

MARCH						
M		4	11	18	25	
Tu		5	12	19	26	
W		6	13	20	27	
Th		7	14	21	28	
F	1	8	15	22	29	
Sa	2	9	16	23	30	
Su	3	10	17	24	31	

APRIL						
M	1	8	15	22	29	
Tu	2	9	16	23	30	
W	3	10	17	24		
Th	4	11	18	25		
F	5	12	19	26		
Sa	6	13	20	27		
Su	7	14	21	28		

MAY						
M		6	13	20	27	
Tu		7	14	21	28	
W	1	8	15	22	29	
Th	2	9	16	23	30	
F	3	10	17	24	31	
Sa	4	11	18	25		
Su	5	12	19	26		

JUNE						
M		3	10	17	24	
Tu		4	11	18	25	
W		5	12	19	26	
Th		6	13	20	27	
F		7	14	21	28	
Sa	1	8	15	22	29	
Su	2	9	16	23	30	

JULY						
M	1	8	15	22	29	
Tu	2	9	16	23	30	
W	3	10	17	24	31	
Th	4	11	18	25		
F	5	12	19	26		
Sa	6	13	20	27		
Su	7	14	21	28		

AUGUST						
M		5	12	19	26	
Tu		6	13	20	27	
W		7	14	21	28	
Th	1	8	15	22	29	
F	2	9	16	23	30	
Sa	3	10	17	24	31	
Su	4	11	18	25		

SEPTEMBER						
M		2	9	16	23	30
Tu		3	10	17	24	
W		4	11	18	25	
Th		5	12	19	26	
F		6	13	20	27	
Sa		7	14	21	28	
Su	1	8	15	22	29	

OCTOBER						
M		7	14	21	28	
Tu	1	8	15	22	29	
W	2	9	16	23	30	
Th	3	10	17	24	31	
F	4	11	18	25		
Sa	5	12	19	26		
Su	6	13	20	27		

NOVEMBER						
M		4	11	18	25	
Tu		5	12	19	26	
W		6	13	20	27	
Th		7	14	21	28	
F	1	8	15	22	29	
Sa	2	9	16	23	30	
Su	3	10	17	24		

DECEMBER						
M		2	9	16	23	30
Tu		3	10	17	24	31
W		4	11	18	25	
Th		5	12	19	26	
F		6	13	20	27	
Sa		7	14	21	28	
Su	1	8	15	22	29	

RELAX & UNWIND

TV's finest hour

Comedy historian Robert Ross takes a trip to Walmington-on-Sea to uncover the origins of the Home Guard battalion known as Dad's Army

In Hope and Glory (1987), John Boorman's nostalgic celebration of his wartime childhood, there is a moment of pure farce. The old boys of the Home Guard stumble down the street, much to the amusement of onlookers. But this scene is less of reality and more of collective shared memory of a comedy show. For, by the late Eighties, Dad's Army had crystallised forever in our national consciousness.

As genuine memories of those dark days of the Blitz and the Buzz Bombs, rationing and Vera Lynn fade into history, the slapstick silliness of Walmington-on-Sea is omnipresent.

Silly maybe, but sincere and sensitive too, Dad's Army is not only among our most cherished television, it's also a carnivalesque salute to our finest hour.

Perfect theme tune

The Second World War had been over for 23 years when the inaugural episode of Dad's Army, The Man and the Hour, was transmitted on July 31, 1968.

Every element is fully formed: from Arthur Lowe's bumptious portrayal of bank manager-cum-army-captain George Mainwaring, to that pitch-perfect signature tune recorded by veteran comedian Bud Flanagan.

Bud may have taken his final curtain call during the recording schedule for the second series, in October 1968, but his heart-breaking vocal refrain became synonymous with the series and was retained throughout.

Certain Dad's Army fans labour under the misconception that Who Do You Think You Are Kidding Mr Hitler? must have been a Bud Flanagan and Chesney Allen hit from back in the Forties. But no. It sounds authentic, largely thanks to Bud's effortless delivery and the fact that Jimmy Perry, the song's co-writer and series co-creator, was steeped in the traditions of music hall.

It was Perry who came up with the notion of a Home Guard series in the first place.

He had been the original "stupid boy" when, during the war, aged 17, preciously mollycoddled and living the life of Private Pike, he was stationed with a troop of old soldiers in the 10th Battalion in Watford, Hertfordshire. He met all sorts of characters and they would all end up in Dad's Army, filtered through his obsession with the great variety comedians of the day.

John Laurie, the dour Scots undertaker Private Frazer, with his oft-repeated lament of: "We're doomed!" had been playing that cantankerous personification of foreboding for decades. There are shades of Frazer in Laurie's performances for Old Mother Riley's Ghosts and The Ghost of St. Michael's (both 1941), opposite Will Hay.

The three-way clumsiness and intricate wordplay of authoritative Will Hay, the aged Moore Marriott and fresh-faced Graham Moffatt, in a glut of earlier films at Gainsborough Pictures, begat Mainwaring, Godfrey and Pike. There was more than a little of comedian Robb Wilton's naive and effete ponderousness about Sergeant Wilson; while sharp-suited and fast-talking Private Walker was straight out of Sid Field's Slasher Green spiv act or 'Prince of the Wide Boys' Arthur English.

They Don't Like It Up 'Em!

Indeed, Arthur English was originally in the frame to play Walker as an older man, before James Beck was cast as a much younger, slick draft-dodger. Much to Jimmy Perry's initial chagrin: he had originally written the role for himself!

It wasn't the only bit of hasty re-casting. Even as early as the late Sixties, 28-year-old David Jason had been specialising in playing old men, subsequently in service of mentor and champion Ronnie Barker as the curmudgeonly Lord Rustless.

Thus, Jason was in the frame to don white whiskers once more as the befuddled Corporal Jones. That was until Clive Dunn,

another actor well known for playing older than his years, got the role instead, and would happily shout: "They don't like it up 'em!" for the whole run.

Jon Pertwee, just before landing a career-defining role as the third face of Doctor Who, had been heavily tipped to play Sergeant Wilson. Jon's cousin, Bill Pertwee, however, kept it in the family playing the bellowing Air Raid Warden... "Put that light out!"

Like the legendary BBC Radio wartime comedy sketch

The slapstick silliness of Walmington-on-Sea is omnipresent

---

show I.T.M.A. (It's That Man Again), Dad's Army was full of catchphrases, many of which have now entered the national lexicon.

Michael Mills, Head of Comedy at the BBC, had commissioned the show.

Perry's original title, The Fighting Tigers, was changed, characters were tweaked and added, and the razor-sharp

David Croft was assigned to oversee the project. As co-writer, director, producer and a leader of men, it was a decision that made situation comedy history.

Dad's Army would run to nine series, until November 1977. Nearly a decade of laughs, and at least 34 months longer than the Second World War.

In that time too, there were radio adaptations, a children's annual, a West End musical revue, an extensive theatre tour and a feature film, all with the majority of the core Magnificent Seven in place.

In the intervening years, Dad's Army has not only remained one of the constants of BBC programming, but an entire cottage industry of merchandise and spin-offs have kept the brand buoyant. There are tin mugs and greetings cards, plush toys and woollen socks, remakes and reboots.

With a perfect ensemble cast, sublime writing, dollops of slapstick, a soundtrack of genuine Forties favourites and an unwavering sense of feel-good community, Dad's Army is as much a part of our way of life as fish 'n' chips and moaning about the weather.

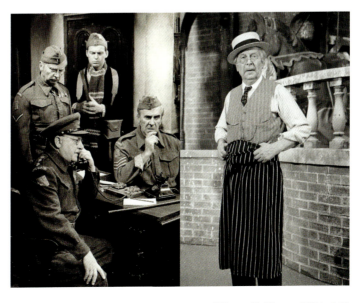

QUICK CROSSWORD 1

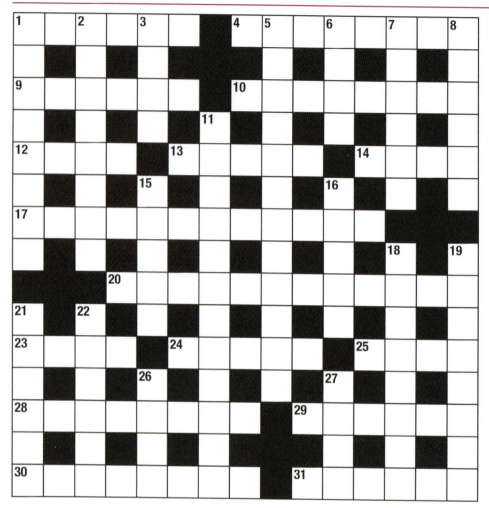

ACROSS
1 Morally bad (6)
4 Educated guess (8)
9 Continue to be (6)
10 Mechanic (8)
12 Misleading ploy (4)
13 Ransack, rummage (5)
14 Glance over (4)
17 Weighty metal device formerly attached to prisoners (4, 3, 5)
20 Author of a film script (12)
23 Slightly open (4)
24 Alloy of iron and carbon (5)
25 Flat circular object (4)
28 Territory (8)
29 Globe (6)
30 Woman's warm-weather garment (8)
31 Without charge (6)

DOWN
1 Cupboard for clothing (8)
2 Short negligee (8)
3 Touch of - - -, Orson Welles film (4)
5 Unaided (6-6)
6 Exotic wader (4)
7 Business providing a specific service (6)
8 Wandering (6)
11 Cry of annoyance (12)
15 Emerge from an egg (5)
16 Day-by-day account (5)
18 Vociferous (8)
19 Savoury biscuits often eaten with cheese (8)
21 College land and buildings (6)
22 Wild West bar (6)
26 Fibber (4)
27 Unaggressive fight (4)

Puzzles

QUIZ 1

Go Figure

Each answer is a number which corresponds to a letter eg 1=A, 2=B and so on. When you have all six numbers, rearrange the corresponding letters into the word that has a connection to one of the questions.

1	2	3	4	5	6	7	8	9	10	11	12	13
A	B	C	D	E	F	G	H	I	J	K	L	M

14	15	16	17	18	19	20	21	22	23	24	25	26
N	O	P	Q	R	S	T	U	V	W	X	Y	Z

1 To be eligible to stand as a member of parliament in the UK, a person must be at least how many years old?

2 How many series were produced of the ITV detective drama Endeavour?

3 At birth, a baby elephant can weigh 120kg, that is almost the equivalent of how many stone?

4 Complete the title of this 1903 collection of poems by English writer and poet Rudyard Kipling – The ____ Nations?

5 How many players are there in a traditional curling team?

6 On most computer keyboards there are how many function keys?

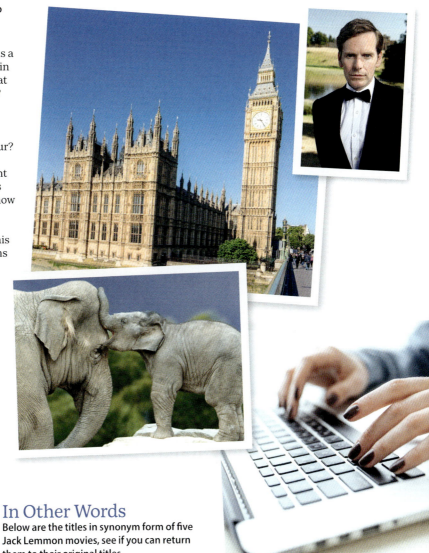

In Other Words

Below are the titles in synonym form of five Jack Lemmon movies, see if you can return them to their original titles.

1 Absent
2 Away Directed Toward Expanse
3 Papa
4 Conflagration Descending Beneath
5 Bronco

Were you right? Turn to page 182 for the answers

Driving Me Crazy

Pearl is waiting anxiously for some news and tries to keep herself busy at home, but her thoughts keep returning to her grandson. Will there be cause for celebration or commiseration?

By Holly Anne Crawford

Pearl took the cake from the oven, put it on the worktop and smiled as the aroma filled the kitchen. While waiting for it to cool, she scampered into the lounge to check everything was in place.

The 'congratulations' card sat on the table alongside a gift secured with a blue ribbon. She'd positioned them next to the vase so they could be swept out of sight if it was bad news. Then she chided herself for thinking negatively.

Pearl fiddled with the tablecloth, moved the chairs and then peeked at the clock. She frowned. Has it stopped?

She put an ear to it. No, it just felt like time was standing still.

Stifling a yawn, she returned to the kitchen for a coffee, only to discover she'd already made one. Her mind was all over the place. She'd hardly slept and was up before the birds had uttered the first note of the dawn chorus.

She began pacing the hallway. Then, worried she'd wear the carpet out, went upstairs to change. "Surely they should be back by now?" she muttered, using the window reflection to adjust her hair.

As Pearl fiddled, her gaze landed on the front garden and she was horrified to see weeds among her roses. "I'm not having that," she huffed and shot out to deal with them, but her heart wasn't in it.

Back inside she busied herself plumping sofa cushions but was distracted by the photo of her grandson on the mantelpiece. The frame had been a birthday present from Billy. The words 'Best Grandma', picked out in silver, always made her smile.

"How on earth is he old enough to drive?" she muttered. It seemed like only yesterday she'd held him as a newborn and gasped at how much he looked like his Daddy, with blue eyes and a shock of red hair.

As Pearl held him, it felt as if time melted away and she was 18 again and cradling her own baby. He'd grabbed her finger with his tiny hand and her heart melted.

Her husband, John, kissed her head, his eyes shining with pride. "Hello new Mummy," he had whispered.

It took a moment for her frazzled brain to process her new title. 'Mummy.' It felt strange but wonderful. Resting her head on John's shoulder, Pearl rocked their baby.

The pram they'd saved for was Pearl's pride and joy. She'd stroll down the street even when she didn't need any shopping just to show off her son in it. And when people cooed over 'gorgeous baby George' she almost burst with pride.

Her thoughts were interrupted by memories of her grandson's gurgling. She smiled, tears in her eyes.

Once again John had kissed her head. "Hello, Grandma," he whispered, eyes shining mischievously. Her new title sounded odd, but Pearl loved it.

As a toddler, Billy was into everything, especially cars.

Pearl's rug still bore the scars from when he'd used it as a racetrack. "Nanny, I'm winning," he'd squeal, pushing his toy car ahead of hers excitedly.

When her daughter-in-law returned to work, Pearl decided to learn to drive so she could help out by taking Billy to nursery or on trips.

In the blink of an eye, Billy was a schoolboy, all smart in his uniform. Then a teenager, always tinkering with machinery. But he always made time for his grandparents. And at 6ft tall, he towered over his petite gran.

"Nan, you may be small, but you're mighty," he'd say, tucking into a homemade delicacy.

"And you make mighty great cakes too!"

Pearl's thoughts were interrupted as the driving school car pulled up. She squealed and rushed to the

---

Stifling a yawn, she returned to the kitchen for a coffee, only to discover she'd already made one

---

door, trying to read Billy's face as he approached, "Well...?"

He looked at her with sad eyes and then broke into a grin.

"He passed!"

Pearl hugged him.

"Is this a private party or can anyone join in?" John asked, appearing behind them.

"Congratulations, darling," Pearl gushed.

John threw his 'L' plates in the air and triumphantly shouted, "A new driver, passing my test at 70. Not bad, eh?"

Pearl was delighted that John had accepted and passed the challenge she'd set as his eighth decade approached.

"Me, learn to drive, don't be daft," he'd scoffed when she'd

suggested it over breakfast one day. "You can't teach old dogs new tricks."

"Course you can," she said, buttering toast. "I didn't pass until I was in my forties."

"That's different," he'd retorted. "You never let anything stop you."

She knew why he was hesitant. John liked routine and detested change.

He'd never learned to drive because he hadn't needed to. He'd stayed in the village where he'd been born and walked to the farm where he worked.

If he needed to go further afield he'd get on his bike, or, if push came to shove, the bus. Though he always insisted that 'shanks's pony' was the best form of travel.

Indeed, he'd walked to the funfair the night he met Pearl. He won her a coconut and they held hands all the way home. They'd been together ever since.

But retirement never suited John. So when Billy started his own driving school, Pearl booked her husband a block of lessons.

"That'll keep him out of mischief," Billy said. "I'll even give you a family discount."

"You're all heart," Pearl had giggled.

Later, as Pearl cut the celebratory cake, she took her chance.

"Darling, now you've passed, you can be my chauffeur. It's only fair after all these years of me driving you... and we can go on that driving holiday because we can both get behind the wheel."

John's eyebrows shot up. "But it's not like it'll be a new experience. After all, I've been driving you crazy for years."

Pear smiled. "It's a good job I 'wheely' love you, then."

With that, she took a big bite of cake and congratulated herself on putting her family on the road to success.

On the inside

Half a century after it arrived on our screens, Porridge is regarded as TV comedy gold. Chris Hallam goes behind the cell doors of Slade Prison

No other sitcom of the time had an opening sequence quite like Porridge. Viewers were exposed to the stark, cold reality of convicted criminal Norman Stanley Fletcher's journey into his new 'home' as he takes up residence at what was then referred to as Her Majesty's Pleasure: Fletcher (Ronnie Barker) is an inmate in Slade Prison.

There was no theme tune (at least not until the show's end). Instead, Fletcher's arrival is punctuated only by the psychologically crushing sound of the heavy prison doors being closed behind him.

We also hear the words of Fletcher's sentencing judge (delivered in a voice that is also recognisably Barker's) as they echo around his head. He is a "habitual criminal", a man who sees arrest and imprisonment as "an occupational hazard". Fletcher still looks decidedly uneasy, licking his lips anxiously as he faces up to the prospect of five long years inside…

Best of British TV

Seven of One

The word was out: Ronnie Barker was on the lookout for a new sitcom. It was the early Seventies. Barker was in his mid-40s, well-known for shows such as The Two Ronnies. But he wanted more.

As a result, in the spring of 1973, a series of comedy pilots entitled Seven of One was broadcast, each featuring Barker as a different character, or characters, in a variety of situation comedy scenarios.

This exercise was to prove a triumph. While five of the pilots aired, the first two evolved into Barker's two biggest-ever sitcom successes. The first, written by Roy Clarke, was Open All Hours. The second, Prisoner and Escort, was written by Dick Clement and Ian La Frenais, best known as the creators of The Likely Lads.

It was based around two prison officers, the steely Mackay (Fulton Mackay) and the gentle, mild-mannered Henry Barrowclough (Brian Wilde) as they transported Barker's compulsive criminal, Norman Fletcher, to the remote (fictional) Slade Prison.

In Barker's hands, the potentially unsympathetic character of 'Fletch' became instantly loveable. "I'm only in prison because of my beliefs," he admitted. "I believed the night watchman was asleep." Prisoner and Escort became Porridge. The first series started in September 1974 and ran for 21 episodes until March 1977.

Going down

Barker originally envisaged a set-up similar to the US Army-based series, Bilko. But as he and the writers visited a number of increasingly grim prisons as part of their research, it was soon recognised that a darker approach was needed.

One brilliant move was the creation of a younger character who the more experienced

and cynical Fletcher could help. Lennie Godber was only intended to be a minor role (he is not in the pilot at all), but Richard Beckinsale quickly proved such a natural that he soon became a star. Barker had suggested Paul Henry (later Benny in ITV soap, Crossroads) for the part, but was happy when Beckinsale was cast and the two established an easy

---

In Barker's hands, the unsympathetic character of 'Fletch' became loveable

---

rapport. Beckinsale was already known for his role opposite Paula Wilcox in The Lovers. His run as Alan in Rising Damp tallies almost exactly with his time in Porridge.

Porridge was an immediate hit, amassing viewing figures close to the 18 million mark.

Breaking out

Always wary of becoming typecast, in 1977 Ronnie Barker decided to quit: "I always worried about getting stuck with a character. I didn't want that."

Writer Ian La Frenais later regretted this. "I think we should have pressed Ronnie and we should have pressed ourselves to do more," he said. "I think Porridge is definitely a series short. It was ridiculous for something that popular to only do the three series."

It was not quite the end for Fletch and Godber, however. The year 1978 saw the two going it alone in the outside world in Going Straight. The spin-off saw Fletch running into his old rival Mackay, and Godber marrying Fletch's daughter, Ingrid (Patricia Brake). But it was never as popular as Porridge.

Then, in 1979, Porridge returned for a final film version, released in the US under the name Doing Time. Although not a bad film in itself, the release was overshadowed by the news of the tragic death of Beckinsale who died of a heart attack soon after filming ended at just 31.

In 2003, Barker came out of retirement to play an elderly Fletcher in spoof documentary, Life Beyond the Box. Barker died in 2005 but always retained fond memories of Porridge. "It was probably the best and most important show I did," he said.

Fear of Flying

Rose is determined not to let her fear of flying stop her from meeting her first grandchild

By Linda Sainty

R ose turned over and reached for her mobile on the bedside table. It was almost three am, which meant it would be nearly midday in Melbourne, and she was sure she'd heard it ping. But there were no new messages on her WhatsApp.

Must have imagined it, she thought with a sigh.

"I wonder when this baby's going to make an appearance," she muttered to Malc through the darkness, grabbing the pillow from his empty side of the bed and cuddling it close.

He didn't answer.

"Why don't you go downstairs and make yourself a nice cup of tea?" she heard Malc's voice in her head.

"Good idea," she whispered back, getting out of bed and throwing on her dressing gown to keep her warm against the cold night air.

Her nocturnal wanderings were not unusual these days. Everything had got out of kilter in the past few months.

A short time later she was sitting at the kitchen table under the harsh glare of the ceiling light, drinking tea and eating a cheese sandwich. Odd behaviour, she realised, for a woman who used to be meticulous about not eating between meals.

She picked up her mobile and scrolled through recent photos on it. They were mostly of Tia, her heavily pregnant daughter who was expecting her first baby, Rose's first grandchild, in less than three weeks.

Tia had moved to Australia two years ago, when she got the opportunity of a secondment to work at the Melbourne branch of her firm.

The placement was only for a year but she met and fell in love with Adam, and now they had bought a home together and were expecting a baby.

"How are you doing?" Rose texted, hoping Tia wouldn't realise she was phoning her in the early hours of the morning.

A few moments later a reply came back. "Good! But what are you doing up at this hour?"

"Drinking tea and eating a cheese and pickle sandwich," Rose answered.

"Mum, are you OK?" Tia texted back, adding a concerned looking emoji.

"Fine," she answered. "But what about you? Any developments on the bump front?"

There was a short silence then suddenly her phone rang and they were talking instead of texting.

"She's quite comfortable in there, I think," Tia was saying. "Too comfortable. I'm as big as a bus and feel as if I've been pregnant forever. And it's unbearably hot."

"Don't make me jealous, it's unbearably cold here. Typical February weather," said Rose. "But I know how you're feeling. You were a week overdue and I felt as if you'd never arrive." She bit her lip. She was meant to be giving her words of encouragement, not making her feel worse.

"But I'm sure everything will be fine," Rose went on breezily. "When I was near my due date me and your gran would go on long walks together, which at least helped pass the time, even if it didn't make you arrive any earlier."

"I wish you were here, Mum," Tia was saying with a sigh, "then we could go on long walks together".

Rose felt a lump in her throat because she wished that too, but knew that it was an impossibility.

She'd always hated the idea of flying and the thought of spending long hours high in the sky sitting in a big metal capsule filled her with dread. That's partly why Tia and Adam had enjoyed two weddings. One in Australia and one in the UK.

Which, as it turned out, was fortuitous because Malc, who had been unwell for some time, suddenly took a turn for the worse and wouldn't have been able to travel.

"I wish I could be with you too," Rose was saying, "but, unlike you and your dad, I've never been brave enough to fly."

"I know you don't like flying," said Tia. "But you're brave in other ways, Mum," she assured her. "You were brilliant looking after Dad at the end.

And he told me you nursed me through whooping cough when I was tiny. That must have been really scary."

She'd forgotten about Tia catching whooping cough when she was a baby and all the sleepless nights she'd spent looking after her. Fancy Malc remembering that!

"Well, you just get on with things." Rose shrugged, "it was

> **"When I was near my due date me and your gran would go on long walks together, which at least helped pass the time"**

---

no big deal. As for your dad, you know what he was like, always the joker, always upbeat."

An image of Malc and Tia waving from a rollercoaster as she stayed firmly on the ground, staring upwards in wonderment and terror at their daring, suddenly shot into her mind. She'd always hated heights.

Suddenly she felt emotional. Her feelings came in waves. "I think I'd better go to bed," she told Tia with a yawn. "Get some beauty sleep. Speak soon."

"Love you, Mum."

"Love you too."

The next morning as she was making a cup of tea, Tia's words pinged into her brain. I wish you were here, Mum. We could go on long walks together.

And she knew what she had to do: somehow overcome her fear and get on a plane.

There was no time to waste. There were things to sort out; a visa and flight tickets to book. Not to mention packing her suitcase and making sure she put in summer clothes and the outfits she had bought for the new baby.

New baby! Suddenly joy surged through her. It was so exciting to think she would soon be meeting her granddaughter. Tinged with sadness that Malc wouldn't get to see her, or the sights of Melbourne, which he would have loved.

He always enjoyed visiting new places and if it hadn't been for her flying phobia, she knew they would have gone on lots of holidays in far-away places.

In a way she was doing this for the two of them and she hoped he would be proud.

As she sat down with her cup of tea, she heard Malc's voice in her head. "What next, Rose? A bungee jump?"

QUICK CROSSWORD 2

ACROSS
1. Spiny plant (6)
4. Junior Girl Guide (7)
10. Crime of stealing (7)
11. Flammable gas (7)
12. Rapid (4)
13. Affectionate name for a parent's mother (4)
14. Staggers drunkenly (5)
16. Forceful rebuke (6)
17. Go in separate directions (7)
21. Gulp (7)
22. Support at a time of distress (6)
25. Room on a boat (5)
27. Statement of money owed (4)
28. Bird-watcher's hut (4)
30. Express delight (7)
31. Skilled conductor (7)
32. Kate Middleton's title (7)
33. Insufficient amount (6)

DOWN
1. ITV series about couples in Manchester that starred James Nesbitt and Fay Ripley (4, 4)
2. Spiral shape (9)
3. Second-hand (4)
5. Sentimental (8)
6. Large colourful fruit (10)
7. Furious (5)
8. Stretchy fabric (5)
9. Strap for controlling a dog (5)
15. Bizarre (10)
18. Warrior in an amphitheatre (9)
19. Rubbish! (8)
20. Gigantic beast (8)
23. Tally (5)
24. Sudden decline (5)
26. Elegant but small (5)
29. Yield (4)

QUIZ 2

Go Figure

Each answer is a number which corresponds to a letter eg 1=A, 2=B and so on. When you have all six numbers rearrange the corresponding letters into the word that has a connection to one of the questions.

1	2	3	4	5	6	7	8	9	10	11	12	13
A	B	C	D	E	F	G	H	I	J	K	L	M
14	15	16	17	18	19	20	21	22	23	24	25	26
N	O	P	Q	R	S	T	U	V	W	X	Y	Z

1 How many episodes were produced in the three series and specials of Ben Elton's BBC2 sitcom Upstart Crow starring David Mitchell as William Shakespeare?

2 How many times has the Argentina national football team won the World Cup?

3 How many eyes does a wasp have?

4 The British bank Lloyds was founded in the year 176_?

5 How many cities are there in Scotland?

6 On a standard dartboard, which number sits between two and three?

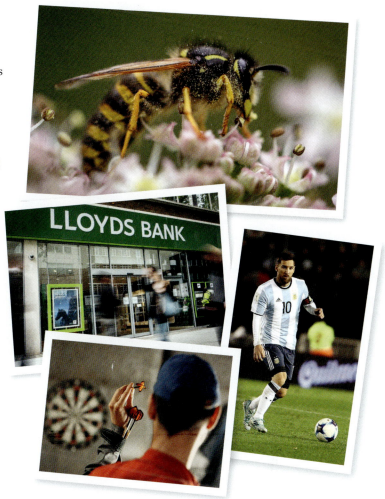

In Other Words

Below are the titles in synonym form of five classic novels, see if you can return them to their original titles.

1 Journey
2 Arrogance Exposition
3 Perception Along with Responsiveness
4 Cache Atoll
5 Miniature Females

Were you right? Turn to page 182 for the answers

A House with a History

James and his wife may have found their dream home, especially as it comes with a tragic mystery that crime writer Ellie can't resist

By Daria Davis

"I do hope it's haunted." Ellie Marsh looked up at the rambling stone house, overgrown with ivy.

"You hope everything's haunted, dear," said her husband James with a smile. "My wife's a crime writer," he explained to the estate agent. "Can never have too much atmosphere."

"There's no resident ghost, if that's what you mean." The agent, a slight, middle-aged man with a perpetually tired expression, unlocked the door and frowned. "Of course, there was the incident..." He paused, as if unsure whether the "incident" qualified.

"Oh yes?" Ellie's eyes lit up with a glow James privately referred to as "unholy". "Do go on, Mr Charlton, we'd love to hear about it."

Mr Charlton waved them into an elegant entrance hall dominated by a wide staircase.

A thick layer of dust somewhat marred its grandeur, but Ellie gasped in delight at the period details visible beneath the grime.

"It's not been lived in for a while," said their guide apologetically. "The couple who were here before only had the house for two months. I'm afraid it ended in tragedy. She was found dead at the foot of these stairs, and her husband was arrested for murder."

"Good lord!" James exclaimed, just as Ellie murmured, "How interesting".

"At first it looked like an open-and-shut case," continued the agent. "All the doors and windows were locked up for the night, and there were only two sets of keys. Mrs Allerton's were still in her handbag in the kitchen. The husband had his with him when he went out to play pool with a friend."

"He had an alibi?" said Ellie.

"So it appeared. Witnesses in the pub claimed that Allerton was there from 7pm. He left at around nine. It would have taken him 15 minutes to walk home and, at 9.20pm, the police received his call. He sounded genuinely distressed."

Ellie ran a fingertip along one of the windowsills, trailing a cloud of dust.

"What time did Mrs Allerton die?" she asked.

"The estimate was between eight and nine."

"That does seem to let out Mr Allerton."

"Hold on," put in James. "Isn't it possible she simply fell down the stairs?"

The agent shook his head. "She didn't fall. She was shot."

Ellie positively twirled in delight, spreading her arms out as she took in the grand hall.

"A locked room murder! My favourite." She drifted through to the drawing room, asking questions as she went.

"Was the gun ever found?"

"Oh yes, lying right beside her. It was Allerton's gun, which he kept in his study. No fingerprints, but that's not surprising."

"And he had a motive?"

"Mrs Allerton had a large sum of money from her divorce a few years previously. Apparently she'd cleaned out her first husband and married her boyfriend. Allerton was several years younger than her."

"So everything points to him. Motive, opportunity... drat, if only he didn't have such a good alibi!"

"But he was arrested," pointed out James. "So they must have found something on him. Go on Ellie, let's see if you can find the missing piece."

Ellie stopped abruptly and plopped down on a silk-upholstered sofa.

"Were there other suspects?" she asked.

"Mrs Allerton's ex-husband was interviewed, but he was working late that night and had clients who could vouch for him. The cleaner had been in that day, but she left around five and went home to her family. As they were new to the neighbourhood, there wasn't really anyone else to interview."

"It must be the husband," said James. "It always is in your books, at any rate."

"Nonsense, dear," murmured Ellie absently. "In the last one it was the butler, as per tradition."

She jumped up and walked through to the kitchen. The two men followed, watching her open drawers and peer into cupboards. She seemed completely absorbed in the kitchen arrangements, though James knew that underneath her brain was busy working out the details of the crime.

After a while Mr Charlton cleared his throat.

"Can you really figure out how Allerton did it?" he asked tentatively.

"Oh yes," Ellie murmured, engrossed in testing the oven settings. "That is to say, I know how you framed him."

She stopped fiddling and gave the agent an apologetic smile. "I hope you don't mind me saying."

James gaped at the two of them.

> **"The couple who were here before... I'm afraid it ended in tragedy. She was found dead at the foot of these stairs one evening"**

"You're telling me the murder – you... " He stepped protectively in front of Ellie, who patted him on the arm.

Remarkably, the little agent only nodded.

"How did you know?" he asked.

"Oh that's easy," said Ellie, nudging James aside. "The husband's alibi was simply too good. And if no one else had a key, then the whole thing would be impossible.

So there must have been another set of keys, which naturally made me think of an estate agent." She gestured around her in illustration.

"Especially when you mentioned the woman's ex-husband, who was busy with clients in the evening. He was the only other suspect, and he had quite the motive."

"And his alibi?" asked Mr Charlton with a slight smile.

"An estate agent comes and goes between viewings. That kind of alibi is easy to fake with clients timed around the crime."

James looked from his wife to the agent in utter confusion.

"If it was you, why on Earth would you tell us what you'd done?" Ellie gave him a loving oh-Watson look.

"I don't think he's done it yet, dear," she explained. "We can't be the only couple interested in the house. My guess is that Mrs Allerton came here with her new husband, maybe not so much to look at the property as to gloat at her ex. That's when he got the idea. Revenge on both husband and wife, but it had to be foolproof. And then he saw our names on the viewers' list and thought, why not get the crime writer to test solve the problem? Isn't that right, Mr Charlton?"

The agent made a funny little bow of acknowledgement.

"You've got it exactly, Mrs Marsh. You're even cleverer than your series detective." He sighed. "I am sorry for trying to use you to straighten out the kinks in my plan."

"I make lots of drafts too," she said sympathetically. "They're a devil to get right."

"Can we just return to the small matter of murder, please?" asked James irritably. "You won't be... trying the real thing, will you Mr Charlton?"

"I think he's learnt his lesson," said Ellie. "In any case he can hardly kill the woman without the two of us coming forward and telling the police what we know. Best just forget all about it," she finished brightly, and strode back towards the entrance hall, the two men following in her wake.

"Now, how about you show us the rest of the house, Mr Charlton? I get the feeling I just might like to buy it."

Perfectly Frank

When it comes to physical comedy, no sitcom star went to more dangerous extremes than Michael Crawford as Frank Spencer in Some Mothers Do 'Ave 'Em, says Douglas McPherson

"You couldn't have it today, because of Health & Safety," said Michael Crawford of the show that made him famous, Some Mothers Do 'Ave 'Em.

First broadcast more than 50 years ago on 15 February 1973, the sitcom followed the mishaps of the accident-prone Frank Spencer and became as famous for its high-risk stunts as its slapstick comedy and much-impersonated catchphrases, including "Ooh, Betty, I've had a bit of trouble!"

Clad in Frank's distinctive beret, tank top and raincoat, Crawford did all his own stunts, whether roller-skating under a moving articulated lorry or hanging from a rope beneath a helicopter high above a Norfolk church in a 50mph gale.

Because the interior scenes were shot in front of a live audience, Crawford had to get the stunts right first time so that when he, for example, rolled down a staircase knocking out all the bannisters, the audience would react with genuine surprise.

Even some of the stunts filmed on location, such as Crawford driving a Hillman Imp off the end of a pier, had to be shot in a single take because they only had one car to wreck.

Sometimes things went wrong, including the time Crawford was hanging from a window cleaner's cradle 200 feet up an office block.

His bodyweight tipped the cradle against the building, jamming it, which meant he was stuck there for 20 minutes.

Crawford's daredevilry impressed even the show's stunt arranger, Stuart Fell.

Recalling the iconic sequence in which Frank roller-skated down a flight of steps and shot off a pavement to end up hanging on to the back of a moving bus, Fell said: "That was all Michael. He should get the credit as a stunt arranger."

A real cliffhanger

Another memorable moment saw Crawford dangling from the bumper of a Morris Minor that was teetering precariously on the edge of a cliff. Fell has since revealed that the car was fixed to hinges anchored to a pair of railway sleepers dug into the ground, so that it could be tipped back and forth.

"There was no chance of that car going over the cliff," said Fell, who dangled from the bumper to test it the day before Crawford filmed.

He nevertheless stacked a pile of boxes at the foot of the cliff as a crash pad in case anyone took a tumble.

Fell donned a red polka dot dress ready to stand in for Frank's long-suffering wife, Betty (Michele Dotrice), in a sequence where the couple crawled over the see-sawing car's roof. But Dotrice opted to do the stunt herself, a pair of hands holding her ankles out of shot. "It was a bit hairy," Dotrice recalled. "But I loved doing it and got whipped up in the enthusiasm of Michael."

Dotrice's mother though was unimpressed. After watching the episode, she slapped her daughter and said: "How dare you do something so silly!"

Some Mothers Do 'Ave 'Em was the first commissioned work from Raymond Allen, a cinema cleaner in Shanklin on the Isle of Wight. "I started writing for television when I was 15 and didn't sell anything until I was 31, and that was Some Mothers," he told his local paper, the Island Echo, in 2016.

In some ways, Allen was the real-life Frank Spencer. He accidentally flooded the cinema while cleaning the toilets and drove a car into a ditch during a driving lesson.

"A lot of it was based on myself," he admitted. "I tend to drop trays and break things and I'm always walking into things that have just been painted."

Even Frank's trademark raincoat was based on Allen's.

The writer thought it made him look like Humphrey Bogart until he overheard producer Michael Mills telling a wardrobe assistant to kit Frank out with clothes from a second-hand shop. As a pointer, Mills said, "Take a look at what Raymond's wearing." Allen was too embarrassed to wear it again.

Allen's original script was a one-off play about Frank wrecking a hotel room on his and Betty's honeymoon. Having never earned more than £10 a

The show was an immediate hit, drawing 26 million viewers at its peak

---

week, Allen was astonished to be offered £350 an episode to write a complete series.

His cinema colleagues were equally astounded. When he told them he was going to work for the BBC in London, one replied: "You'd think they'd have enough cleaners of their own."

Ooh, Betty!

Dotrice's casting as the patient, down-to-earth Betty helped to ground Frank's antics in a sense of reality. She was just as much of a rock to Crawford off screen, supporting him during his divorce. He called her the sister he never had.

The show was an immediate hit, drawing 26 million viewers – or around half the population of the UK – at its peak.

But after just three series, it bowed out in typical daredevil fashion with Crawford (a real-life pilot) performing aerial acrobatics as Frank took flying lessons in a 1978 Christmas Day special watched by 19 million.

Refusing to be typecast, Crawford returned to the stage with starring roles in Barnum and Phantom of the Opera.

In 2016, the 74-year-old strapped on Frank's rollerskates once more to appear with Dotrice in a one-off episode of Some Mothers for Sport Relief.

"I'm more than delighted with the legacy," said Crawford. "You dream of success like that. You never imagine it will happen to you."

The show's impact was too big for its creator to follow, however. Allen went on to write for Little and Large, Frankie Howerd and others, but never sold another sitcom.

"It was a bit disappointing," he reflected in later life. "They'd say, 'We liked the script, but it wasn't as funny as Some Mothers Do 'Ave 'Em'."

Killing Time

Cliff is dreading the thought that his wife may have planned a surprise party for his 60th birthday

By Michael Donoghue

Cliff wasn't expecting to spend the morning of his 60th birthday in the park, sheltering from the rain.

It was down to his wife, Hilary, that he was there. After breakfast, she'd casually suggested that a leisurely stroll around the park for a few hours would do him good. Cliff raised an eyebrow. Did she want him out of the house? Suppressing a smile, he put on his coat and headed out.

He'd only just walked through the gates when the heavens opened.

Looking round frantically for somewhere dry, he was relieved when he saw the canopy that overlooked the boating lake at the end of the path. Hurrying towards it, he sat himself down on the bench beneath and caught his breath.

Cliff checked his watch. It was now half past 11. Peering out just then, he saw his mate, Fred, hurrying up the path, shoulders hunched, with his dog at his side. Calling out, he waved him over.

"Nice weather for ducks," Cliff remarked as they dashed under the canopy.

"Alfie here needs walking come rain or shine," Fred sighed, shaking his coat.

"What are you doing here – apart from the obvious?"

"Killing time," Cliff sighed, scratching Alfie's ears. "It's my birthday today, and my wife's thrown me out of the house. Said I can't go back until one o'clock."

Fred frowned. "You can't stay here 'til then." He looked at the sky. The rain was finally easing. "Why don't we both kill some time in the King's Head? I'll buy you a birthday drink."

"Cheers, mate," Cliff grinned, as they headed towards the gates.

"Perhaps your wife's planned a surprise party for you?" Fred suggested as they sat down with their pints, Alfie stretched out under the table.

Cliff shook his head furiously. "She knows I don't want one of those. Being put on the spot – very embarrassing."

Fred rolled his eyes. "Since

when do women listen? When they get an idea into their heads there's no stopping them. If your wife's anything like mine, that's what she'll have done; you mark my words."

When Cliff thought about it, Hilary had been acting strangely, even before this morning – and so had their daughters, Amy and Emma.

The hushed phone calls over the last few weeks, their whispered conversations as they sat on the sofa...

"You're right," he said, finishing his pint. "She wanted me out of the house so she could set everything up. And I bet our girls are there helping her. It all makes sense now."

Fred raised his eyebrows. "Prepare yourself for the inevitable, mate."

Cliff looked nervous. "If I'm going home to a surprise party, then I need some Dutch courage." He picked up their empty glasses. "Same again?"

When Cliff left the pub at quarter past one, he was a little the worse for wear. As he turned into his street, he spotted both his daughters' cars parked outside the house.

So there is a party, he thought as he reached the gate. Then he wondered why they hadn't come by taxi if they were going to be drinking...

Cliff expected to see balloons and glittery banners on the front door and up at the windows. But there was nothing displayed to suggest that it was his birthday.

Listening intently, he couldn't hear any sound either.

When he let himself in, Hilary stepped into the hallway. "There you are," she smiled.

"If I'm going home to a surprise party, then I need some Dutch courage"

"We were wondering where you'd got to."

"We?" Cliff said, pretending to be surprised.

"Many happy returns, Dad," Amy and Emma said in unison as he walked into the lounge.

"Happy birthday, Grandad!" four mini voices chorused as two boys and two girls rushed to greet him.

Cliff smiled at them all. Looking round, he was relieved to see that there were no guests gathered, and no buffet on the table.

Though he was surprised to see a sheet of wrapping paper covering the mirror above the fireplace.

Hilary stood by it. "Happy birthday, dear," she said, and kissed his cheek.

"Aren't you going to remove the paper, Dad?" Amy grinned.

Curious, Cliff tore it off – and couldn't believe his eyes. Mounted to the wall was a large flat screen TV.

"What on earth...?"

"It's from all of us," Hilary said, "and it's tuned in and ready to watch. What do you think?"

Cliff was speechless.

"Sorry, Dad, but we had to get you out of the house while it was installed," Emma added.

"And that was where your mate, Fred, stepped in," Hilary explained.

Cliff's eyes widened. "He knew about this?"

"Yes – and I see he kept you occupied," she chuckled. Then she added: "As you didn't want a party, I've ordered us a takeaway for this evening. We can eat it while we sit and view in style."

Cliff grinned. "I can't think of anything I'd like better."

QUICK CROSSWORD 3

ACROSS
3 Official in charge of mail distribution (10)
8 Flying or hovering at altitude (6)
9 Accident and emergency department (8)
10 Eccentric (8)
11 Method (6)
12 Spectator (8)
15 Lose hope (7)
17 Powerful military rank (7)
19 Evaluator (8)
21 Stable for hire (6)
25 Additional text at the bottom of the page (8)
26 Neckerchief (8)
27 Not quite (6)
28 One who is feeling dozy (10)

DOWN
1 Codeword for S in the phonetic alphabet (6)
2 High-kicking dance (6)
3 Plots of land or buildings (10)
4 Chunk (7)
5 Thin fog (4)
6 Marine animal (8)
7 Appetiser (6)
11 Broadcasting and magazine industries (5)
13 Rapt (10)
14 Car race (5)
16 Appraise prematurely (8)
18 Vulgar (7)
20 Scribble messily (6)
22 Thug who causes damage (6)
23 Baby's noisy toy (6)
24 Jealousy (4)

Puzzles

QUIZ 3

Go Figure

Each answer is a number which corresponds to a letter eg 1=A, 2=B and so on.
When you have all six numbers rearrange the corresponding letters into the word that has a connection to one of the questions.

1	2	3	4	5	6	7	8	9	10	11	12	13
A	B	C	D	E	F	G	H	I	J	K	L	M
14	15	16	17	18	19	20	21	22	23	24	25	26
N	O	P	Q	R	S	T	U	V	W	X	Y	Z

1 Complete the title of this 2001 American cop action thriller movie starring Robert De Niro & Edward Burns: _ Minutes?

2 Koalas may sleep between 18 and how many hours a day?

3 At sea, when the current is at its strongest a whirlpool can be up to how many metres deep?

4 A Lorry can have up to how many forward gears?

5 The normal top speed of a worker bee, when travelling unladen is roughly between 15 to how many miles per hour?

6 How many Carry On movies did actress Joan Sims feature in?

In Other Words

Below are the titles in synonym form of five Rolling Stones songs, see if you can get some satisfaction by returning them to their original titles.

1. Upright
2. Buffoon Directed Toward Weep
3. Sepia Carbohydrate
4. Disaster Along with Despondency
5. Larger Error

Were you right? Turn to page 182 for the answers

Pale Lemon 4-Ply

Lorna is angry with her son Ollie until something transports her back to a time when he was a tiny baby

By Susan Wright

I didn't mean to get side-tracked when we went to the pound shop. I'd told my husband that we'd rush in, get some padded envelopes, and rush out again, and that's what I'd intended to do. But I found myself stopping dead when I came across the display of knitting wool half way down the store.

"Goodness," I breathed as Dave stopped too. "I didn't know they sold wool in here. They've got some beautiful colours, haven't they?"

"Yeah, lovely," Dave agreed, unenthusiastically.

"I love this," I said, reaching out to touch a ball of pale lemon 4-ply. "I knitted Ollie a cardigan in that colour when he was a baby, didn't I?"

"Yes, you did." Dave said before swiftly changing the subject. "Anyway, we came in here for padded envelopes. Where do you think they are?"

I looked around and shrugged. "I've no idea, but..."

"I'll go and see if I can find someone to ask," Dave interrupted, glancing at his watch. "We need to get back to the car park, so you stay here and I'll find out where they are."

"Yes, OK," I said as he started walking away and my eyes were drawn to the wool again.

The lemon 4-ply was so pretty and, as I stared at it, I pictured the knitting pattern I still had at home and remembered how I'd sat in an armchair in our first house, knitting that cardigan for Ollie.

It had been the only thing I'd ever knitted, but I'd been so proud of it, and Ollie had looked adorable in it with his red hair.

We had some photographs of him wearing that cardigan. He'd been so sweet back then. People had often smiled when they'd set eyes on him, and we'd taken hundreds of snaps of him.

The photographs were all stuffed in a drawer now though. We hardly ever looked at them anymore, but every now and then I would take them out and let myself wallow in the memories and, funnily enough,

---

> ## "I touched one of the balls of wool again and felt something inside me melt"

I'd looked at the old photos just the night before.

Not the baby ones though. I'd sat and stared at pictures of Ollie in his first school uniform. He'd looked so smart in the grey trousers and the royal blue sweatshirt, and I'd been so proud of him when he'd started school.

Reading and writing had come easy to him, so he'd sailed through his primary school years with glowing reports, and things hadn't been much different when he'd gone on to secondary school.

He'd always been gifted, so it had been obvious that he would go to college and university, and we'd never worried about the expense because he was our only child.

A much-loved child. A child who'd been conceived after I'd suffered six miscarriages. A child I'd never dared believe that I'd have until I'd held him in my arms.

When the labour pains had started, I'd gripped hold of Dave's hand and convinced myself that something would go wrong, but Ollie had been a perfectly healthy baby, although he was premature.

He'd changed our lives and grown into a lovely young man. A young man I'd been proud of – until he'd come home from college a month before and told me that I was going to be a grandmother.

"You what?" I'd gasped.

"Sarah's pregnant." He grinned.

"Pregnant?" I repeated incredulously. "But... but what about university?"

He shrugged. "I won't be able to go. I'll have to get a job instead."

"But you were going to do a maths degree!"

"So?" He looked me in the eye. "I honestly don't care, Mum. I know you wanted me to go to university, but..."

"But how can Sarah be pregnant." I stared at him in astonishment.

"How do you think?" Ollie rolled his eyes and let out a sigh.

"Look, I know it's a shock, but Sarah and I are thrilled, and I thought you'd be pleased too."

"Pleased?" I yelled.

"Yes, pleased," he'd muttered, staring at the floor so he didn't have to look me in the eye.

He'd looked just like a kid again. And I'd stood there and screamed at him while poor Dave had tried to mediate. My anger hadn't altered anything, though.

A month on, Ollie was still adamant that he and Sarah were going to have the baby, and equally adamant about quitting his education and getting a job.

He hadn't budged an inch and neither had I, and we hadn't spoken for weeks.

But as I stood there in the pound shop and saw Dave hurrying towards me, waving some padded envelopes, I touched one of the balls of wool again and felt something inside me melt.

"Right, let's go and pay," Dave said.

"In a moment," I said, picturing Ollie's cardigan. "I won't be a second, Dave. I just want to get some wool."

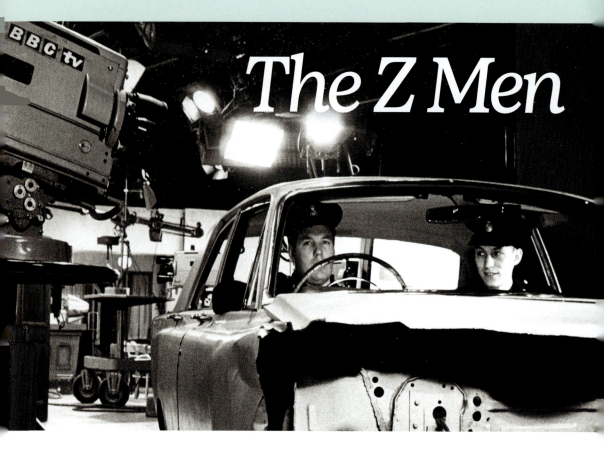

The Z Men

With one of the most hummable themes in TV history, Z Cars heralded the arrival of a gritty new cop show. Douglas McPherson recalls the stars and cars

More than 60 years ago, on January 2, 1962, the nation settled down to watch a new police drama. The show opened at the graveside of a murdered constable, where DCI Barlow (Stratford Johns) and Sergeant Watt (Frank Windsor) were discussing the replacement of 'Bobbies on the beat' with 'Crime patrol' cars to tackle escalating problems on local estates. From there we cut to the home of PC Bob Steele (Jeremy Kemp) the morning after he'd given his wife a black eye in a row over his drinking.

Z Cars ushered in a new era of gritty cop shows that came in shocking contrast to the cosy tone of its predecessor, Dixon of Dock Green. The unvarnished portrayal of police work so upset the Chief Constable of Lancashire, where the series was set, that he wrote to both the BBC and the Home Office to try to get it banned.

Viewers loved it, however, and the show ran until 1978, making household names of its cast, including Brian Blessed, who answered to the indelible call sign, 'Z Victor 1' as PC 'Fancy' Smith.

The programme was conceived by the BBC as a rival to Coronation Street and Emergency Ward 10 on ITV, and did its job, pulling in 14 million viewers in its first season. The programme would never have come about, however, if scriptwriter Troy Kennedy-Martin hadn't gone down with the mumps. To take his mind off his illness, he tuned into the police radio channel.

"I came across incidents where it was obvious that the police were not coping," he remembered. "They seemed confused, lost, apparently young and inexperienced.

"The world that filtered through these fragmented calls was so different from that of Dixon that I took the idea for a new series to Elwyn Jones, who was the head of a small but influential section of the BBC

Drama Department." The series' police advisor was Detective Sergeant Bill Prendergast whose real-life casebook had inspired the BBC's four-episode comedy drama Jacks and Knaves, in 1961. With 30 years of frontline experience, Prendergast showed the programme makers a side of day-to-day policing – and policemen – that more senior officers would have preferred the public not to see.

Gritty real life drama
In the era of kitchen-sink drama, Z Cars dealt with contemporary social issues such as the migration of working class families from inner-city slums to soulless estates with no sense of community. It often featured low-key crimes, such as pub fights and pickpockets.

The emphasis was on the characters, especially in one episode where the officers spent their whole shift talking because they had no crimes to tackle!

To give the show a documentary feel, producer David Rose cast screen unknowns led by Johns, who came out of the 'angry young man' school of theatre at London's Royal Court.

Within four weeks, however, Blessed said: "You couldn't walk down the street – we were as famous as The Beatles! The country waited for every episode."

Although it featured some location filming in the Merseyside town of Kirkby, the series was mostly transmitted live from Studio 6 at the BBC Television Centre in London. "The terror of performing live gave the show its vitality," said Colin Welland, who played PC David Graham. "And it was great, because you came off stage and everyone had seen it. The bin man the next morning would say, 'That was a good 'un."

The spin-offs
Z Cars merchandise included a children's annual, a softcover Z Cars – Meet The Stars Special and, of course, scale models of the show's trademark Ford Zephyrs.

When the original series ended in 1965, the central double act of Barlow and Watt transferred to the fictional area of Wyvern, near Bristol, for spin-off series Softly, Softly, and then to the Essex-like 'Thamesford' for Softly, Softly: Task Force. Johns was also given his own series, Barlow at Large (later retitled Barlow) that ran from 1971 to 1976.

Z Cars ushered in a new era of gritty cop shows... in contrast to Dixon of Dock Green

---

In the meantime, Z Cars returned as a twice-a-week programme in 1967, with the original series' PCs Bert Lynch (James Ellis) and Jock Weir (Joseph Brady) leading a mostly new cast. By the time the series ended on September 20, 1978, Lynch had risen to the rank of Inspector. The final shot showed him with a sad look on his face, symbolically rolling down the electric shutter at the front of the police station.

By that point, the once ground-breaking series was looking tame compared to ITV's abrasive new cop show The Sweeney, which was, ironically, created by Kennedy-Martin's brother, Ian.

Z Cars will always be fondly remembered as staple viewing in the Sixties and Seventies, however, and paved the way for later police procedural The Bill.

Arresting music
With its stirring fife and drums, the Theme From Z Cars remains one of the most evocative TV theme tunes of its era. Based on the 19th century Liverpool folk song Johnny Todd, it was arranged for the show by the husband and wife team of Fritz Spiegl and Bridget Fry.

By April 1962, the show was so popular that a recording by Norrie Paramor and His Orchestra reached No.33 on the chart, while a jazzier competing version, arranged and conducted by Johnny Keating, reached No.8.

James Ellis, who played PC Lynch, also released a vocal version, with the lyrics of Johnny Todd, although his version didn't make the charts.

Sound Judgement

*Marguerite discovers that a good
amateur detective doesn't just look for
clues, she listens for them as well*

By Laird Long

"I'm sorry this weekend has been so distressing, Marguerite," Trevor Bannister apologised again, gazing glumly at his old friend seated across the living room of his large country home. "I'd hoped this would be a nice, quiet weekend – just the two of us."

He gestured angrily at the ceiling. "And it would have been – if they hadn't shown up."

It was midnight. Trevor's uninvited offspring, Brandon, Bruce and Beatrice, had just trooped up the staircase to the second floor bedrooms; after yet another heated exchange with their estranged father. The trio could be heard banging around upstairs, getting ready for bed.

"Well, it's been… interesting," Marguerite offered with a smile.

"Quarrels all day long. They're concerned that I might change my Will and that they'll miss out on their inheritance. I warned them this afternoon that if they don't all change their ways, I might just cut them off now without a penny. I hope that's given them something to think about.

"It hasn't been peaceful, that's for sure. Even at night we can't get any peace. Brandon snoring, Bruce tossing and turning in his sleep, and Beatrice yelling at the pair of them to be quiet because she's a 'light sleeper'. I should've stuck them in the sheds out back."

Marguerite set down her teacup and rose to her feet. "Well, I think I'd better go up to bed myself, Trevor. Perhaps I can even get to sleep before the symphony starts up."

Trevor jumped out of his chair, spry for a man his age, and took hold of his friend's hand. "I'm truly sorry for all the commotion, Marguerite. I know it's been trying for you."

Marguerite patted the man's hand. "I've enjoyed all the fresh air, the beautiful countryside, and the delicious food. And your company most of all, Trevor."

He returned her warm smile.

A loud bang woke Marguerite from a blessed sound sleep an hour-and-a-half later. She sat up in bed, listening, but she didn't hear anything else.

She slipped out of bed and into her dressing gown, and padded over to open the door of the bedroom. She peered down the darkened hallway.

All seemed quiet. As Marguerite's eyes adjusted to the dark, she saw Trevor's bedroom door was ajar. She tip-toed out of her room and down the hall and looked into her host's bedroom.

Trevor Bannister was sprawled out on his back on the floor of his bedroom. Marguerite could see the bullet hole in his forehead from the doorway.

"Crime scene? Are you saying that Father was murdered?"

After confirming that her friend was indeed dead, Marguerite left the bedroom and headed back down the hallway to her bedroom to grab her mobile phone and call the police. While punching in the number for Inspector Blackburn in the nearby village she decided to take a look into each of the other bedrooms.

There she saw Brandon lying on his back with his eyes closed, breathing rhythmically, apparently peacefully asleep; Bruce lying on his side, also motionless and sleeping quietly; and Beatrice curled up under her bed covers. All appeared oblivious to the shocking events that had just happened.

Marguerite turned on the lights in the hallway and her bedroom and made her phone call. Then she knocked loudly on each of the other bedroom doors in turn. Trevor Bannister's daughter and two sons roused themselves and stumbled out into the hall, rubbing their eyes.

"I'm sorry to have to tell you that your father's dead," Marguerite stated. "The police are on their way." She noted little emotion in the faces of the trio at the news.

"None of you heard a gunshot?" she asked.

"No, I've been asleep," was the response repeated by each of the siblings.

Brandon moved towards the closed door of his father's bedroom, but Marguerite stopped him. "That's a crime scene," she said. "Not to be disturbed."

"Crime scene? Are you saying that Father was murdered?" Beatrice asked.

"That's exactly what I'm saying," Marguerite replied grimly. "With all three of you having a hand in it."

The murdered man's estranged offspring gaped at Marguerite.

"What on earth makes you think that?" Bruce demanded to know.

Marguerite explained, so all could hear. "You each claim to being asleep when your father was shot. But based on what Trevor told me, and my observations when I looked into your rooms just now, none of you were actually asleep."

She looked at each of them in turn. "Brandon, the snorer, was dead quiet. Bruce, the tosser-and-turner, was dead still. And for a light sleeper, Beatrice appeared to be dead asleep, despite the loud gunshot that awakened me in my room at the end of the hall."

Before the trio could take any further deadly action that night, Marguerite heard a most welcome sound from downstairs – the police pounding on the front door of the house.

QUICK CROSSWORD 4

ACROSS

1 Act of rescuing ships (7)
5 Inscription on a tomb (7)
8 Worker who creates shop displays (6-7)
10 Unfermented soya-bean curd (4)
11 Soft and hairy (5)
12 Tense (4)
15 Dilapidated home (5)
16 European language (9)
18 Poetic word for 'maybe' (9)
19 Plastic flooring material (5)
21 Intense anger (4)
22 Neat tower of objects (5)
24 Currency token (4)
27 Get one's wires crossed (13)
28 Sagged (7)
29 Deprived part of a city (4, 3)

DOWN

1 Term in prison (7)
2 Simplistic rule regarding probabilities (3, 2, 8)
3 Skin complaint (4)
4 Darwinian theory (9)
5 Senior person (5)
6 Entry on a list (4)
7 One with nonconformist beliefs (7)
9 Automatic payment from a bank account (8, 5)
13 First Greek letter (5)
14 Relinquish (5)
17 Activities for keeping fit (9)
18 Solid shape with triangular sides (7)
20 Archery implement (7)
23 Take a step (5)
25 Simple card game (4)
26 Exclusive Indonesian holiday destination (4)

Puzzles

QUIZ 4

1	2	3	4	5	6	7	8	9	10	11	12	13
A	B	C	D	E	F	G	H	I	J	K	L	M

14	15	16	17	18	19	20	21	22	23	24	25	26
N	O	P	Q	R	S	T	U	V	W	X	Y	Z

Go Figure

Each answer is a number which corresponds to a letter, eg 1=A, 2=B and so on. When you have all six numbers, rearrange the corresponding letters into the word that has a connection to one of the questions.

1 How many championship grass tennis courts are there at Wimbledon's All England Club?

2 How many movies did legendary Hollywood couple Spencer Tracy and Katharine Hepburn star in together?

3 A tiger can jump vertically up to how many feet?

4 In 1999, Keep on Movin' became the first UK number one for which pop group?

5 Complete the title of this 1985 TV movie starring Peter Ustinov as detective Hercule Poirot: __ at Dinner?

6 'Einundzwanzig' is the German word for which number?

In Other Words

Below are the titles in synonym form of five Glenn Close movies, see if you can return them to their original titles.

1 Serrated Rim
2 Curved Residence
3 Volte-Face Appertaining to Opulence
4 Deadly Allure
5 Prompt Clan

Were you right? Turn to page 182 for the answers

Kindred Spirits

When a neighbour agrees to take care of a sick woman's dog it awakens something that had been long forgotten

By Ian Joynes

I loved this place once, a long time ago. I used to visit here every day, in all weathers, come what may. This was where I regularly got sunburnt, muddy, sodden to the core, yet never once cared, for this verdant bit of open space was a taste of freedom for me, somewhere I could feel the breeze blowing freely through my hair, and spend time decluttering my mind.

This patch of unkept heathland, not far from home, gave me a chance to start each day afresh, to press life's pause button, and take a break from the trite concrete landscape doing its best to suffocate me. I solved many of my life's dilemmas along these pathways.

But above all else, I came here each day for my dog, Bess, to set her free, watch her running around as mad as a March hare, unrestricted by her lead. Like me, she loved it here, so many scents and interesting places to stop and explore, her tail wagging furiously at everyone we met. They say that dogs don't smile but, like me, Bess always smiled whenever she came here.

Bess was my best friend, a cross collie, full of fun and energy, excited by everything she ever came across. I loved that precious dog dearly with all my heart. She was so much more to me than a canine, and we shared so many happy adventures together.

But sadly, nothing in life is forever. Bess got older and her wagging tail eventually fell still. I'll never forget that day when part of me died with her, nursing her in my arms at the vet's. Even now my eyes mist with tears at the mention of her name. She was irreplaceable, and I swore I'd never have another because of it, choosing instead to live the rest of my life by myself. But when my neighbour, Betty, fell ill and moved into a hospice, my life changed again without me having any say in the matter.

"Promise me that you'll look after Coco until I get better again," she begged, but poor Betty never did get better. I think she knew. But I'm glad I could provide her with the comfort of knowing that Coco was going to be taken care of.

Coco was a young chocolatey brown mixture of all sorts, with matching chocolate buttons for eyes. I'd patted her on the head many times when seeing them out and about together, never once thinking that soon she'd be living with me... a woman in her fifties and very much set in her ways.

But if I hadn't promised, then Coco would have ended up in a rescue centre, far too young to be abandoned and given up on. Looking into her sad velvety brown eyes, I knew instantly that I could never do that to her.

I'm still not sure whether I adopted Coco, or whether she adopted me, but I'm pretty sure she's happy with the situation now. She came with her own bowl, lead and basket, but I wouldn't have had the heart to let her use the things I still had hidden away in the cupboard

that once belonged to Bess. Coco was nothing like her predecessor. She had her own mischievous little personality, and could sometimes be a proper little madam, but obedient and faithful too.

We soon got to know each other, which were her favourite foods and treats, and that my slippers were not for chewing.

Coco put a smile back on my face that had been missing for a long, long time. It was a new beginning for us both.

For the first few weeks, whenever we went out, I kept Coco firmly by my side on the lead. I needed to make sure she was comfortable with me, and would come back when I called her if she got free.

Finally, it was time to give a new lease of life to my wellingtons; they'd not been muddied in a long while.

I decided that today was the day I was going to take her to where I used to bring Bess, and let her run free. I was probably more excited than she was as

we crossed the road together. I'd not been here in years, but I could feel my heart racing as we reached the other side.

I was more than a little apprehensive as I let her off the lead for the first time. She looked up at me with grateful eyes, and was soon running ahead amongst the humming bees and butterflies with her tail wagging furiously at every smell and sound.

> **"Coco put a smile back on my face that had been missing for a long, long time"**

Watching her run free was such a beautiful thing. We were both happy as I momentarily stopped to take in everything around me – the birdsong, blossom and sweet smell of the outdoors that I'd missed so much.

But then suddenly I realised she was gone. I awoke from my daydream with a start,

my mind in torment. Coco had disappeared. She'd been there just in front of me only moments ago, but now there was no sign of her, and we were closer to the main road than I would have liked.

"Coco!" I yelled at the top of my voice, to no response.

"Coco!" I shouted again in an air of a panic and whistling shrilly too.

Scanning around me, all was quiet, where could she possibly have gone? Those few mad seconds seemed like hours as I repeatedly shouted her name.

And then they appeared. Yes, both of them. Coco and Bess together. They were cavorting through the long grass and flowers, tails wagging and barking with the sun on their backs.

I come here every day again now with Coco, in all types of weathers, just to watch her and Bess running freely through the fields together, two kindred spirits, and both as mad as March hares.

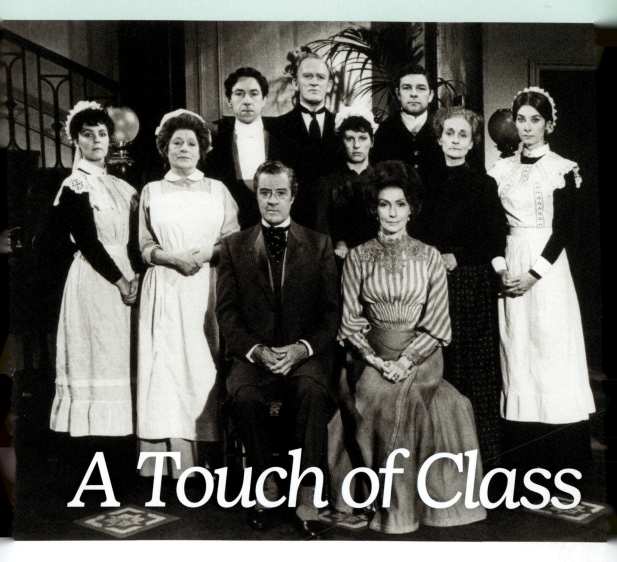

A Touch of Class

A drama about the lives of an aristocratic Edwardian family and their staff, Upstairs, Downstairs proved to be a surprising hit

Few expected much of Upstairs, Downstairs. LWT's head of drama, Cyril Bennett, didn't. "It's pretty but it's just not commercial television," he predicted. "They'll switch off in their thousands." The series was thus delayed considerably before its final TV debut, over 50 years ago in October 1971, and even then it was buried in what seemed to be the 'graveyard' slot at 10pm on Sunday – a spot usually reserved for sneaking out anything expected to flop without anyone noticing.

But Bennett turned out to be very wrong. Upstairs, Downstairs was not a flop. People started watching. Indeed, by the time the final episode was aired just over four years and 68 episodes later, just before Christmas 1975, it had become an award-winning success. It was one of the biggest British TV shows of the decade and is still fondly remembered as one of the greatest series ever made.

Back in time

The opening episode of Upstairs, Downstairs took viewers back to November 1903, a time which, in 1971, was still within living memory for many older viewers. Audiences met chirpy Sarah (Pauline Collins) as she applied for a position as a parlourmaid at 165 Eaton Place, a typical upper-class

Edwardian house with a team of 'downstairs' staff who looked after the 'upstairs' family led by MP Richard Bellamy (David Langton) whose wife, Lady Marjorie (Rachel Gurney) was destined to go down on the Titanic in 1912.

By the end of the first series, which took in events up to 1908, viewers had become familiar with memorable characters, including Scottish butler Mr

---

In time, the series would be watched by 300 million people in 50 countries

---

Hudson (Gordon Jackson), cook Mrs Bridges (Angela Badderley), stern head parlourmaid Rose Buck (Jean Marsh), Welsh valet and chauffeur Thomas Watkins (John Alderton), and rakish son of the house, James Bellamy (Simon Williams).

It had all started as an idea dreamed up by two friends,

Jean Marsh and Eileen Atkins. Both were actresses in their 30s, and naturally keen to create opportunities that might provide them with work.

They originally envisaged a comedy called Behind the Green Baize Door in which they would play two Victorian housemaids. The idea evolved.

The comedy element was dropped, the setting moved forward in time and the name changed to Below Stairs. An 'upstairs' family was introduced, as Marsh observed, "servants have to serve somebody". In the end, Atkins was unavailable to act in the series but Marsh took on the role of head parlourmaid, Rose Buck.

Many of the episodes of what became Upstairs, Downstairs were written by different people. The first was credited to novelist Fay Weldon. In time, the series would be watched by 300 million people in 50 counties. Over four years, viewers saw the household move through a

quarter century as the setting moved from the Edwardian era, the First World War, the Roaring Twenties up to the start of the Great Depression.

The final episode

For all its success, by the end of the fourth series, many of the cast (including Jean Marsh) were keen to move on to other projects, so it was decided the fifth series, which covered the period from 1919 up to 1930, would be the last. In the final episode, 165 Eaton Place was sold and Rose wandered around the empty house, remembering times past.

A number of Upstairs, Downstairs spin-off series were proposed. In the end, only one, Thomas and Sarah, was produced in 1979. This followed the adventures of Pauline Collins' and John Alderton's characters after they left the household at the end of the second series of Upstairs, Downstairs. It did not repeat the success of the original.

Thirty-five years later, Upstairs Downstairs dropped the comma from the title and moved to the BBC for a full-blown relaunch of the series, now set in the Thirties. An impressive 7.5 million watched its debut on Boxing Day 2010, which starred Keeley Hawes and saw a new family moving into 165 Eaton Place. With many of the original cast by then either dead or in old age, and many viewers too young to remember it anyway, the link to the original was slightly tenuous.

Creator Jean Marsh returned as Rose Buck, but Marsh soon suffered a mild stroke. Co-creator Dame Eileen Atkins also finally took a part as Lady Maud Holland but left the series early on. The revival ended after two series, having proven unable to compete with the original, or with the massive success of the ITV rival, Downton Abbey.

The Writing Group

Gwendoline regrets using the people in her writing group as inspiration for a short story. Now it's been published she needs to try to make amends

By Vivienne Moles

Dear all, please forgive me for not delivering this personally. As you can imagine, I am beyond mortified by this whole situation. I was so chuffed when I received the acknowledgement that my short story, 'Mayhem at the Writing Group', was accepted by Fiction Shorts. It wasn't until I checked my submission afterwards that I realised what I had done. I can only apologise for any embarrassment I might have caused. It certainly cannot match the embarrassment I am feeling right now.

Gabby, it was quite out of order of me to call you a 'nosey old biddy who can't keep her curtains closed'. I know you just like keeping abreast of developments in the area. You make an absolutely brilliant area watch co-ordinator because of how very observant you are. I often hear your praises being sung about what a hands-on parish councillor you are, never afraid to wade in to controversial issues. It is essential that you have strong opinions and follow things through: an admirable quality. I am sorry that the kiddies are shouting 'Gossipy Gabby' every time you leave your house. As for the graffiti I saw on your garage the other day, I felt as though I should offer my services for its removal, but I feared I would not be welcome. I must say, that widened my vocabulary, I can tell you.

Jonathan, I know you like Freda quite a lot, but seem afraid to wear your heart on your sleeve. I do hope this has not put the mockers on it entirely. I am sure it was a completely platonic visit to the cinema back in the summer.

When you write fiction, you usually have to exaggerate a little. Doubtless you weren't 'snogging in the back row like two hormonal teenagers'. We writers sometimes put things in for comedic or dramatic effect. I am sure you will realise that in the fullness of time when Freda starts talking to you again and we can put all this behind us.

Short story

parties have always been such a delight. I had never even heard of an 'amuse bouche' until I came to one of your candlelight suppers. I do hope the invite is still on for next week. I realise I might be pushing my luck there.

Peter, they always say you should write what you know, and I think it is really interesting that you collect milk bottle tops. It is truly amazing the inventive things you have crafted from them, if the three albums of photographs that you showed us here in the group are anything to go by. Maybe it was something you didn't feel ready to share with the rest of the world and I respect that. I am sorry if it has caused a problem. You should write a book about it. I am sure many

> **"I am sorry that the kiddies are shouting 'Gossipy Gabby' every time you leave your house"**

people would want to take it up if they knew how creative you can be with them. Even now, I am trying to get my head round how you made the toy train set out of milk bottle tops and a bit of glue.

This is really all Fiction Shorts' fault as they rushed me ahead of the deadline.

It had been so much easier to form characters from real people that I knew with such different personalities and diverse interests. Of course, I had intended to change a few details, name, gender, age and mix up some of the features. Alas, in my excitement I sent my manuscript off before remembering it wasn't finished, for which I am truly sorry.

Can you ever forgive me my dear friends?

Yours sincerely,
Gwendoline Potterton

Mavis, I know that you appreciate a joke, even if your laugh is 'like a hyena'. At least it is distinctive and we appreciate you have a good sense of humour. I am quite sure you don't need Tena Lady every time Have I Got News For You is on. In any case, there is no shame in it. Those of us who are, shall we say, more mature should stick together. Only others would trivialise it and turn it into a joke. Well, they won't be laughing when they're our age.

Deborah, I count you as one of my dearest friends, and I do hope you realise that I really like your cooking. None of your sponge cakes are ever 'like a pancake that has lost its way' and your biscuits are never 'so soggy it's as though they had already been dunked twice'. Again, dramatic effect. Writing is like drawing a cartoon. You take an aspect and you overstate it until it becomes so exaggerated it is barely recognisable. Your dinner

Puzzle answers

QUICK CROSSWORD NO.1

Page 150

Across 1 Wicked, 4 Estimate, 9 Remain,
10 Engineer, 12 Ruse, 13 Rifle, 14 Scan, 17 Ball and
chain, 20 Screenwriter, 23 Ajar, 24 Steel, 25 Disc,
28 Province, 29 Sphere, 30 Sundress, 31 Gratis.
Down 1 Wardrobe, 2 Camisole, 3 Evil, 5 Single-
handed, 6 Ibis, 7 Agency, 8 Errant, 11 Fiddlesticks,
15 Hatch, 16 Diary, 18 Strident, 19 Crackers,
21 Campus, 22 Saloon, 26 Liar, 27 Spar.

QUIZ NO.1

Page 151

Go Figure 1. Eighteen/r; 2. Nine/i; 3. Nineteen/s;
4. Five/e; 5. Four/d; 6. Twelve/l.
Word SLIDER connected to question 5.
In Other Words 1. Missing; 2. Out to Sea; 3. Dad;
4. Fire Down Below; 5. Cowboy.

QUICK CROSSWORD NO.2

Page 158

Across 1 Cactus, 4 Brownie, 10 Larceny,
11 Methane, 12 Fast, 13 Gran, 14 Reels, 16 Earful,
17 Diverge, 21 Swallow, 22 Solace, 25 Cabin, 27 Bill,
28 Hide, 30 Rejoice, 31 Maestro, 32 Duchess,
33 Dearth.
Down 1 Cold feet, 2 Corkscrew, 3 Used, 5 Romantic,
6 Watermelon, 7 Irate, 8 Lycra, 9 Leash,
15 Outlandish, 18 Gladiator, 19 Cobblers, 20
Behemoth, 23 Score, 24 Slump, 26 Bijou, 29 Cede.

QUIZ NO.2

Page 159

Go Figure 1. Twenty-One/u; 2. Three/c; 3. Five/e;
4. Five/e; 5. Eight/h; 6. Seventeen/q.
Word CHEQUE connected to question 4.
In Other Words 1. Odyssey; 2. Vanity Fair;
3. Sense & Sensibility; 4. Treasure Island;
5. Little Women.

QUICK CROSSWORD NO.3

Page 166

Across 3 Postmaster, 8 Midair, 9 Casualty,
10 Crackpot, 11 Manner, 12 Observer, 15 Despair,
17 General, 19 Assessor, 21 Livery, 25 Footnote,
26 Bandanna, 27 Nearly, 28 Sleepyhead.
Down 1 Sierra, 2 Cancan, 3 Properties, 4 Section,
5 Mist, 6 Seahorse, 7 Entrée, 11 Media, 13
Spellbound, 14 Rally, 16 Prejudge, 18 Profane,
20 Scrawl, 22 Vandal, 23 Rattle, 24 Envy.

QUIZ NO.3

Page 167

Go Figure 1. Fifteen/o; 2. Twenty-Two/v; 3. Five/e;
4. Eighteen/r; 5. Twenty/t; 6. Twenty-Four/x.
Word VORTEX connected to question 3.
In Other Words 1. Respectable; 2. Fool to Cry;
3. Brown Sugar; 4. Doom & Gloom; 5. Biggest
Mistake.

QUICK CROSSWORD NO.4

Page 174

Across 1 Salvage, 5 Epitaph, 8 Window-dresser,
10 Tofu, 11 Furry, 12 Taut, 15 Hovel, 16 Icelandic,
18 Perchance, 19 Vinyl, 21 Rage, 22 Stack, 24 Coin,
27 Misunderstand, 28 Drooped, 29 Skid row.
Down 1 Stretch, 2 Law of averages, 3 Acne,
4 Evolution, 5 Elder, 6 Item, 7 Heretic, 9 Standing
order, 13 Alpha, 14 Waive, 17 Exercises, 18 Pyramid,
20 Longbow, 23 Tread, 25 Snap, 26 Bali.

QUIZ NO.4

Page 175

Go Figure 1. Eighteen/r; 2. Nine/i; 3. Sixteen/p;
4. Five/e; 5. Thirteen/m; 6. Twenty-One/u.
Word UMPIRE connected to question 1.
In Other Words 1. Jagged Edge; 2. Crooked House;
3. Reversal of Fortune; 4. Fatal Attraction;
5. Immediate Family.